250

D1213749

TRIAL BY JURY

>>><<<

*A Complete Guide to the
Jury System*

TRIAL BY JURY

A COMPLETE GUIDE TO THE JURY SYSTEM

Revised

SAMUEL W. McCART
Member, District of Columbia Bar

CHILTON BOOK COMPANY

Philadelphia   New York   London

Copyright © 1964, 1965 by Samuel W. McCart

Second Edition
Second printing, June 1966
Third printing, August 1967
Fourth printing, January 1970

All Rights Reserved
Published in Philadelphia by Chilton Book Company,
and simultaneously in Ontario, Canada,
by Thomas Nelson & Sons, Ltd.

SBN: 8019 1367 5
Library of Congress Catalog Card Number 64-16526
Designed by William E. Lickfield
Manufactured in the United States of America
by Quinn & Boden Company, Inc., Rahway, N.J.

Foreword

"ETERNAL vigilance is the price of liberty." These words are particularly pertinent today when we are witnessing the diminishing freedom of the individual, a development based on the claims of the superiority of the common good over the rights of the individual. The process of erosion applies to all institutions characteristic of our country, including the jury trial system.

It is our purpose neither to defend the jury trial system nor to condemn it. Our purpose is to explain the system fully in a manner easily understood by anyone. So long as understanding is lacking, citizens are unable to form a solid opinion on where to draw the line in the threatening reduction of jury power. Nor are they able to realize the value of the system to them personally.

Until now, there has been no book available to supply this understanding. It is also important that a book be provided which can be used in instructing our young people in the jury system.

THE AUTHOR

Table of Contents

1. How the Jury Trial Began 1
2. America Gets a Jury System 11
3. The Search for Jurors 21
4. The Selection of a Jury 27
5. Criminal—or Civil? 41
6. Actors in the Drama 54
7. The Trial Opens 66
8. What Is Evidence? 72
9. The Defendant's Case 91
10. Directed Verdicts 98
11. The Whole Truth 102
12. . . . and in Closing 108
13. The Judge's Charge 113
14. Inside the Jury Room 120
15. The Verdict 133
16. Jury Power 139
17. A New Trial 152
18. Appellate Courts 155
Epilogue: "How Scrupulously Delicate" . . . 165
Appendix A: Blackstone's "The Nature of Laws in
 General" 169
Appendix B: Instructions Applicable to Criminal and
 Civil Cases 188
Appendix C: Notes on Provisions for Jury Trials from
 State Constitutions 195
Index 199

TRIAL BY JURY

➤➤)❮❮❮

A Complete Guide to the
Jury System

How the Jury Trial Began

MAN alone, among all living creatures, was endowed with the freedom to choose between following his instincts or departing from them. In the exercise of this choice, man learned that departure from the rule of instinct required a substitute rule and that he could not survive in chaos. So that the species could survive, man further learned that he must accept a degree of disciplined restraint—the Law—in choosing to depart from instinct. A single inhabitant of an island has complete freedom. When others are permitted to live on the island, no inhabitant may exercise complete freedom: each must yield some elements of it. In return, each inhabitant acquires assurance of safety in the exercise of the elements of freedom which each retains. Thus, duties and rights become established and observance by all inhabitants of these duties and rights assures the maintenance of peace. The alternative is banishment, servitude, or death for the weaker inhabitants until only the strongest one survives.

The formulation, application, and enforcement of duties and rights constitute rule by law. Disciplined conformity with law is the essential substitute for rule by instinct. Law, then, is not a whimsical imposition of superior authority, but a limitation essential to survival which, by force of the basic law of self-survival, all men should heartily accept and obey.

The word "law" while generally understood, defies simple definition. A definition ample for our purpose is: the rules of conduct which a society develops and accepts as essential for its peace and order; which a society imposes on each member, and to which each member must conform under some penalty for nonconformance. In this sense, law is a rule of action which is prescribed by some power superior to the individual and which the individual must follow.

Obviously, some agency must exist to formulate the law; another to execute and enforce the law; and a third to determine the fact of nonperformance and the penalty to be imposed. These three agencies are spoken of as the legislative, the executive, and the judicial. In our form of government the functions of each are specific and distinct so that no agency controls another, but each acts as a check on the power of the others.

In order to carry out the judicial function, we have a system of courts which have a duty, among others, to settle disputes over our individual rights and obligations to society and to deal out punishment for violation of law, which we call crime. These are the criminal courts. Courts also have a duty to dispose of disputes between individuals involving their personal rights and obligations, their property, or their intangible possessions. These are the civil courts.

The process of settling a dispute by court action, whether the action is criminal or civil, is essentially the same. It consists of three successive steps. The first is to discover, with the greatest possible certainty, the facts connected with the event at issue. The second is to determine the correct law applicable to the facts. The third is to relate the law to the facts and reach a decision as to guilt or liability.

The most difficult step has always been, and still is, to discover or identify the factual situation to which principles of law can be applied. We speak of this step as "finding the facts." There are two methods available to us for finding the facts. The first is to allow a judge to determine the facts, whether alone or with the aid of one or two other judges. The second method is to have a group of laymen, a jury, determine the facts. Both of these methods are used in our trial courts and will continue to be used indefinitely. Whether one method is better than the other is debatable. It is certain, however, that each is preferable under certain circumstances. In this book we deal with the jury trial method but, as a necessary adjunct, we also cover trial by judge rather fully. One who understands trial by jury will also understand trial by judge.

To acquire an understanding of the jury trial system, we need to know how it came into being and how it developed. And as the jury trial system is but one feature of the law, we should have some knowledge of the sources and reasons for the body of law in which it operates.

Law in England did not spring up overnight but was the result of growth through several centuries. When the Roman legions departed from England in the year 407 A.D., they left it to the Celts who had occupied it from time immemorial. Then the Anglo-Saxons invaded and took over, followed by the invasion of the Danes. Finally the Normans invaded in the year 1066. The descendants of these peoples still inhabit England.

Prior to the Norman invasion, a body of law had been developed sufficient to meet the needs of the times. It was based on firmly established usages and customs which qualified as law because they had existed from a time "whereof the memory of man runneth not to the contrary." These laws were not written down but were carried in memory.

There had also developed a system of courts presided over by judges appointed by the sovereign. These judges went from town to town and held court sessions. Each case tried in a court required the judges to find the true usage or custom applicable to the facts presented to them. In this way, the judges determined the validity, scope, and application of the usages and customs which came before them. The determinations of the judges were called decisions.

Each decision on a point of law became a precedent which was expected to be followed in similar cases as they arose. The use of precedents allowed a consistent and uniform law to develop. The Normans brought in the French language and Continental civil law, which is based on Roman law. But neither the French language nor the civil law secured a foothold in England. The system of law by precedent continued.

This development went on despite two handicaps—the many dialects of the people and the high cost of the only available writing materials, parchment and vellum. But by the year 1435, a common language had developed; the art of printing was discovered in 1454; and cheap paper appeared soon after the year 1500. Thereafter, decisions on points of law became available in print and, as before, each decision constituted a precedent.

This body of law is spoken of universally as "the common law." It is to be found in the decisions. For example, if anyone desires to know the rights at common law of a landowner as to trespassers, or to know the time when husbands lost their right to beat their wives at will, one must make a search of decisions and legislation, which might require him to go back to the first printed volumes.

Because the decisions contained the law, common law is sometimes said to be judge-made law. That was not the viewpoint of the early judges. They looked upon their duty as being to *find* the law, in the sense of discovery, and, having found the law, they merely applied it. They did not assume that their predecessors who first found the law applicable to a particular situation were always correct; therefore, they exercised the right to repudiate previous findings which were, in their view, in error.

At the time of the Norman invasion there were two methods of trial. One was by compurgation wherein a person was declared to state the truth if he could get thirty-six men to sign that he was an honorable man. This form of trail was not abolished until 1833. The other method was by ordeal of water or fire. If the person withstood the ordeal, he was regarded to have stated the truth. The Normans brought with them trial by combat, wherein the winning party prevailed at law. This form of trial was abolished in 1819.

The Normans also brought with them the seed of the jury trial system. They used twelve men as a court of inquest to determine title to lands, particularly the land to which the crown could assert ownership. This is the origin of the use of twelve people. Why twelve? An answer—purely legendary—is that the number was in commemoration of the Twelve Apostles.

4

In 1215 came the Magna Charta, as a result of the bitter struggle between King John and his nobles. The king had pillaged and oppressed the nobles, but was legally supported by judges who were appointed by him and were removable at his will. The Charta was signed by King John, twelve barons, and twelve bishops. The provision of the Charta which interests us reads: "No Freeman shall be taken, or imprisoned or be disseized of his Freehold, or Liberties, or free Customs, or be outlawed, or exiled, or otherwise destroyed; nor will we not pass upon him nor condemn him, but by lawful Judgment of his peers, or by (a) the Law of the land. (2) We will sell to no man, (b) we will not deny or defer to any man either Justice or Right."

The Charta, by this provision, has been commonly understood to have established jury trials as a matter of right to all people in England. Actually it did not. This misconception is due to two misunderstandings. The first of these is in reading the word *freeman* as though it meant *free man*. The freemen of that day were the members of the nobility. The common people were known as villeins or villains. They held no free land. The other misunderstanding is in the use of the phrase "law of the land." This phrase was included as a guarantee to the nobility that the right to trial by combat was preserved to them, that their possessions would not be condemned henceforth by arbitrary acts of the king, and that judgment would precede execution. The king could continue to dispense justice to the common people, the nobility were to be tried only by their equals. So, the Charta was a compact between the king and the nobility and did nothing to forward the development of jury trials.

The barons, having been victorious over the king in their assertion of power, took upon themselves to conduct their own courts and to exercise arbitrary power over their vassals and underlings, so that persons not of the nobility were largely denied justice. To correct this situation the first Parliament enacted the Statute of Westminster, the First, in the year 1275. This statute extended the benefits of the just quoted section of the Magna Charta to the common men in these words: "And that no City, Borough, nor town nor any Man be amerced [fined or punished arbitrarily] without reasonable cause, and according to the Quality of his Trespass, that is to say, every Freeman saving his Freehold, a Merchant saving his Merchandise, a Villain saving his Gaynage [his rights in agricultural land, his tools and the product thereof] and that by his or their Peers."

The deep meaning to us of Magna Charta and the Statute of Westminster, the First, is that they established the principle of due process of law. We perpetuate this principle by the Fifth Amendment to our Federal Constitution.

This statute firmly established the King's Courts which went from place to place and held court sessions much as our circuit courts do today. When a court convened, the people of the area were required to report crimes and wrongs committed by villeins in the area, and these suspects were then brought to trial. The jurors, if we can call them such, were twelve men in the area who were most likely to know the facts involved. The losing party could then call for a trial by twenty-four knights. This was the first use of an appeal system in England. If this body decided the case contrary to the verdict of the first jury, the first twelve were subject to attaint; that is, they were subject to a fine which could be extreme to the extent of confiscation of all the jurors' properties.

When it is considered that the jurors were also the witnesses, a finding of attaint was comparable to a finding today that a witness has committed perjury. The threat of attaint must have brought about many verdicts based on expediency.

At this time there were no lawyers in England. It was not until about the year 1300 that Parliament authorized forty men to practice law, that number being deemed sufficient to fill the needs of the country.

The next step in the development of the jury trial system was the hearing of witnesses in open court. We can assume that with the increase in population it became more and more difficult to find twelve men who might know of the doings of their neighbors and know the facts sufficiently well to act as witnesses and jurors. In any event, the use of witnesses in open court was introduced and became established.

So, gradually the jury trial system changed to the form used today. Jurors, instead of being qualified because they *were* to some extent familiar with the facts, changed to men qualified because they did *not* know the facts. This change called for the enactment of statutes covering the qualification and selection of jurors, and it called for the formation of rules of evidence.

The first record of a jury trial conducted substantially as at present is contained in a Year Book of decisions in the reign of Henry IV (1399 to 1413). A writer of the reign of Henry VI (1422 to 1471) describes a jury trial system of that day which is the same as today's—except that jurors with knowledge of the facts were eligible for duty. The system did not prevent the emergence of Star Chamber courts which were in effect from about 1510 to 1603. (Star Chamber courts had extensive criminal and civil jurisdiction, were exempt from the intervention of juries, and could inflict any punishment but death.) During this time, to be accused was to be convicted. This could be so for two reasons: The judges, being corrupted through their subservience to the king, continued to dominate trials even to the extent of restricting juries to evidence acceptable to the judge, and juries feared the wrath of the judges in the use of attaint.

So long as attaint existed there could be no real jury trial, even though there was a procedure of trial similar to that in use today. Attaint finally came to an end in 1670. In that year, a jury sat in a case at Sessions Court involving a charge against two men for unlawful congregating.[1] One of the defendants was William Penn, later the founder of the colony of Pennsylvania. Against overwhelming evidence of guilt the defendants were acquitted. The jurors were immediately found guilty of attaint "in that they did acquit contrary to plain and manifest guilt in contempt of the king and against the direction of the court." Juror Bushell appealed to the Court of Common Pleas. The Chief Justice of that court wrote the historic opinion which abolished attaint.

[1] Bushell's Case, 1, Vaughn's Reports 135 (1670).

It had been a long struggle, beginning when ordinary men escaped, first, from the Normans' ecclesiastical courts, which were notorious for obnoxious prying into the private affairs of families. Defendants next acquired the right to have testimony given in open court under oath as protection against false testimony so that an accuser had to face the accused in court and be tested by cross-examination. They later acquired the means to thwart venal and hostile judges by denying the judge the right to determine the facts according to his fancy and transferred this function to juries made up of their fellow men. They secured the means to thwart tyranny in prosecutions because henceforth the prosecutor had to establish guilt in open court and could no longer rely merely on subservient judges. This was the status of the law regarding jury trials which these ordinary men, these Englishmen, brought to this country.

The long struggle to secure jury trials was based on the desire for impartial trials for those charged with crimes and for those who asserted that wrongs had been committed against them. The struggle, however, did not end when English colonists carried their system of justice to the New World. Trial judges in American colonial courts continued to attempt to dominate juries. Release from this pressure was necessary to finally establish the jury trial system as we now have it.

Two events occurred which effected a radical change. The first event took place in 1734 when John Peter Zenger was prosecuted and persecuted in New York City. This case involved liberty of speech and the freedom of the press to criticize a public official, Governor Crosby.

Zenger, who published a newspaper, was arrested for publishing libelous articles against the governor. New York lawyers did not care to defend him. He finally secured a lawyer from Philadelphia. At the trial, Judge DeLancy ordered the jury to decide whether the publication had taken place—and then *he* would decide whether the writing was libelous. The jury defied him and brought in a verdict of not guilty. Thus was full jury power asserted and exercised. This action was publicized throughout the Colonies and was hailed as a sort of Declaration of Independence that ended judicial domination. It might be said that our present jury trial system reached its fullness at this time—and jury *power* reached the pinnacle of its development in the Zenger case.

The other event was that the writings of a man named Sir William B. Blackstone came into prominence in England in the middle of the eighteenth century. Blackstone was born in the year 1723, and, at the age of fifteen, entered Pembroke College, Oxford, receiving the degree of Bachelor of Civil Law in 1745. He taught at Oxford and became a professor in 1758, then practiced law in London and became a member of Parliament in 1761. Later he was knighted and was appointed Judge of the Court of Common Pleas. He subsequently wrote a complete treatise or textbook of the common law in one hundred and ten sections. It was published in three volumes, the first of which was issued in 1765. These volumes were published under the title *Commentaries on the Common Law*.

This work had phenomenal sales in England—and in the American Colonies. Now there existed for the first time an authoritative statement of the principles of common law which gave a comprehensive and understandable survey of its roots and development. Lord James Bryce, one-time ambassador to the United States, in his great book entitled *The American Commonwealth,*[2] which has been used as a textbook in many colleges, comments on the widespread possession of Blackstone's *Commentaries* by the American colonists. The use of Blackstone's *Commentaries* before and after the writing of the Declaration of Independence accounts for the basic unity of common law in this country, and to it must be given considerable credit for aiding the Founding Fathers in the drafting of our Federal Constitution.

Blackstone must be given great credit for influencing the colonists' attitude toward the jury system. This is what he wrote:

But in settling and adjusting a question of fact, when entrusted to any single magistrate, partiality and injustice have an ample

[2] *The American Commonwealth* (London: Macmillan, 1896).

field to range in; either by asserting that to be proved which is not so, or by more artfully suppressing some circumstances, stretching and varying others, and distinguishing away the remainder. Here, therefore, a competent number of sensible and upright jurymen, chosen by lot from among those of the middle rank, will be found the best investigators of truth, and the surest guardians of public justice. For the most powerful individuals in the state will be cautious of committing any flagrant invasion of another's right, when he knows that the fact of his oppression must be examined and decided by twelve indifferent men, not appointed until the hour of trial; and that, when once the fact is ascertained, the law must of course redress it. This, therefore, preserves in the hands of the people that share which they ought to have in the administration of public justice, and prevents the encroachments of the more powerful and wealthy citizens.

Many of the principles of the common law have been changed since Blackstone's time, but the *Commentaries* are still used as authority on the common law as it existed at the time of the Revolution. (The two latest editions were published in 1959 and 1961.)

In addition to the exposition of the principles of the common law, which was so valuable to judges, lawyers, and laymen, this work contained, as an introductory lecture, a clear and simple explanation of the nature of law. The widespread reading of this explanation was largely responsible for the ability of the colonists to perceive liberty under law and to appreciate its value. Unfortunately, widespread reading of the explanation has not continued, perhaps because it is available only in expensive reprints of the *Commentaries*. It is so valuable in the education of our citizens that it is set forth in full in its original form in this book. (See p. 169.) In reading it, you will understand how the colonists were able to transform references to the English Constitution and Parliament into new instruments of freedom under law—the Constitution and the Congress of the United States of America.

America Gets a Jury System

THE colonists had long been dissatisfied with some of the operations of the colonial courts, and in the Declaration of Independence they expressed two specific grievances against the King regarding the operation of the courts:

He has made Judges dependent on his Will alone, for the tenure of their offices, and the amount and payment of their salaries.
For depriving us in many cases of the benefits of Trial by Jury.

It was to be expected that the colonists would establish a system wherein judges would be free from domination from any source and wherein the right of individuals to jury trial would be firmly established. They accomplished these objectives, and we have them as part of our inheritance.

The Declaration of Independence placed each colony in the position of a sovereign state, though collectively they regarded themselves as a nation. In the four-year period from 1776 to 1780 all the colonies adopted constitutions. This status of sovereignty continued until the newly drawn Federal Constitution was ratified by the ninth colony on June 21, 1788. The other four colonies quickly ratified, and government under the Constitution began on the first Wednesday of March, 1789.

This means that our government is a constitutional government. It is worthy of note that the Federal Constitution was not set up by the states. It was set up, as stated in the preamble, by "We, the people of the United States" and with these specific aims in mind: "in order to form a more perfect union, establish justice, insure domestic tranquility, provide for the common defense, promote the general welfare, and secure the blessings of liberty to ourselves and our posterity . . . ."

Two words stand out in this preamble. The first is the word *justice*. The Constitution does not spell out what is meant by this word, but the framers agreed that the Constitution should be promptly amended to do that. Accordingly, ten amendments, nine of which constitute a bill of rights, were adopted and became effective on December 15, 1791. This bill of rights represents the first time any government spelled out to its citizens the definite rights of the citizens on which the government could not encroach. The word "justice" receives its legal definition in the bill of rights. If a man receives these rights, he receives legal justice.

The other noteworthy word is *tranquility,* meaning that each citizen shall be able to pursue his daily life without disturbance. This is the reign of law.

The Constitution of the United States makes only one reference to jury trials. That is in Article 3, Section 2, Clause 3, which provides that trial of all crimes, except in cases of impeachment, shall be by jury. It makes no provision for jury trial in a civil case. The Fifth Amendment to the Constitution provides that no person shall be tried for a capital, or otherwise infamous crime, unless on a presentment or indictment of a grand jury, and that no person shall be compelled in any criminal case to be a witness against himself. The Sixth Amendment provides for a speedy and public criminal trial. Finally, civil jury trials are covered by the Seventh Amendment, which provides: "In suits at common law, where the value in controversy shall exceed twenty dollars, the right of trial by jury shall be preserved, and no fact tried by a jury shall be otherwise reexamined in any court of the United States than according to the rules of the common law."

These provisions of Amendments Fifth and Sixth apply in federal and state courts. State constitutions have similar provisions.

The Constitution of the United States provides that the judicial power of the United States be vested in a Supreme Court and such inferior courts as the Congress may establish, and it sets forth the jurisdiction of federal courts. The federal court

12

system and the state court systems are entirely distinct, and their jurisdictions, or matters for their determination, are distinct. For instance, the theft and use of an automobile within a state is a state offense. If the automobile is stolen and taken across a state line, the theft is also a federal offense.

The federal courts are in no sense supervisory over the state court systems. The procedure of conducting jury trials in state courts cannot be reviewed in federal courts, except in these two instances: By the Fourteenth Amendment to the United States Constitution, people in the United States cannot be deprived of life, liberty, or property without due process of law. This means that they are entitled to a fair and impartial trial with the right to cross-examine witnesses. By the same amendment, people are entitled to equal protection of the law, meaning that the vital aspects of selection of juries and the manner of conducting trials must apply equally to all people within a state.

The thirteen colonies had operated their courts under the common law and the statute law of England. Therefore, it was but natural that after 1776 the state courts should continue to do so, with limitations. It is commonly said that the states adopted the common law and the statute law of England. That statement is too broad. It is more accurate to say that the states accepted and adopted those principles of the common law and the statute law which affected private rights and rejected those which applied to public law dealing with the administration of government under a King and a Parliament. The constitutions adopted by the new states all provided for the continuation of the right to jury trial.

Under the powers retained by the states, each state legislature may determine the qualifications and method of selection of jurors; the number of jurors who must agree to report a valid verdict; whether the jury is limited to determination of facts or can also determine the law; whether or not the jury can fix sentence, and other details.

The scope of the right to trial by jury is limited to the scope as it existed at the time the state constitutions were adopted, and as that scope may be expanded by constitutional amendment.

13

In this situation, the citizens of each state may alter or abolish jury trials in state courts by amendment to their constitutions.

Each territory or subdivided state later admitted into the Union as a state acquired all the rights possessed by the original thirteen states. Each formed its own state constitution, and these constitutions (except Louisiana's) preserve the right to trial by jury. All adopted the common law except Louisiana. When the United States purchased from France a large area in the western Mississippi Valley under the Louisiana Purchase, the law of France held sway there. The state of Louisiana retains today, to a large extent, the French civil law. This did not provide for jury trials. A jury trial system like that at the common law exists in trial courts by statute, not by a constitution.

The acquisition of Florida from Spain, the union with the originally independent State of Texas, and the acquisition of the area brought in by the Mexican War and the Gadsden Purchase —all these developments resulted in the influence of Spanish law on a large area of the southwest. Some of this influence still persists. However, regardless of the origin of the law in various states, all states have systems of trial by jury.

A few states have codified their laws, including the common law. In these states, the state code replaces the common law. Codes, however, cannot get away entirely from the common law because it is sometimes necessary to consult the common law in interpreting code provisions.

Now we come to a consideration of written or statute law.

Increases in population density in the United States, development of commerce and industry, need for readily acceptable money and currency, need for rules regarding such matters as evidence of debt, shares of stock, sales, and contracts—all these factors have brought forth a vast number of civil enactments by Congress, state legislatures and municipal governing bodies. Enactments by Congress and state legislatures are called *statutes*. Enactments by cities are called *ordinances* but are classed as statute law. If the common law and the statute law are in conflict, the statute law prevails. State statutes must not conflict with either the state constitution or the United States Constitution. Federal statutes must not conflict with the United States Constitution.

Statutes and ordinances have grown in number from the ten laid down by Moses to all sorts of laws dealing with life, liberty, and the pursuit of happiness so that now at almost every turn one is confronted by a law or regulation of some kind. It often happens that a statute merely puts into written form some principle of the common law. At other times, a statute will embody a slight variation from the common law. Or, it may entirely change the common law.

The question of whether an act of Congress, a statute, or an ordinance replaces or abrogates the common law is always a question for a judge to determine. Judges also determine whether a statute or ordinance is constitutional.

Note that statutes and ordinances come into being only after a seeming majority of the people becomes aware of the necessity to check some offensive conduct, or to provide for some new situation. If this evident majority proves by experience to be a large majority, the law is generally acceptable and comparatively easy to enforce. If this seeming majority proves by experience to be a minority, the law is not generally acceptable and is difficult to enforce.

For example, laws prohibiting the sale of liquor on Sundays receive popular support and are not difficult to enforce. In contrast, the law to effect total prohibition was not popular. When the Eighteenth Amendment, prohibiting the making, transportation, and sale of liquor, was submitted to the states, the legislators of the thirty-six states necessary for ratification voted in favor of adoption by eighty per cent of the members. This indicated popular approval. The Volstead Act, which implemented the amendment, went into effect in January, 1920. This law proved to be so unpopular and so difficult to enforce that the Eighteenth Amendment was repealed in December, 1933.

When we speak of "law" or "the law" we mean the combination of the common law and statute law. When combined, they form a pattern of conduct which the community as a whole has determined must be maintained.

Under the common law, a principle was adopted that ignorance of the law is no excuse for a violation of law. (This principle is sometimes stated that every person is presumed to know the law.) This principle was practical and workable under the early common law which was based on the mores of the people. Statute law brought in, and continues to bring in, new and sometimes strange restraints and obligations. It is not possible any longer for an intelligent and educated person to know all statute law—let alone an illiterate or ignorant person. In order to justify a penalty for infraction of a law of which a person is ignorant, it is necessary that the principle of presumption of knowledge be retained. Such an expedient is called a "fiction of law."

Court trials are open to the public except in a few instances. Although attendance by the public at civil trials is small, a sensational criminal trial will often draw a capacity audience. If the audience is disorderly, the judge can have the courtroom cleared. Standees are not allowed. If the evidence may be harmful to morals, minors may be excluded. The fact that trials are public has given rise to a demand for the right to take photographs and to televise trials. These demands will plague the courts for many years.

The form of jury trial in effect when the constitutions were adopted has been defined in these words:

Trial by jury, in the primary and usual sense of the term at common law and in the American Constitution, is a trial by a jury of twelve men, in the presence and under the superintendence of a judge empowered to instruct them on the law and advise them on the facts and (except on acquittal of a criminal charge) he may set aside their verdict if, in his opinion, it is against the law or the evidence.[1]

It should be borne in mind that the state constitutions preserve the right to jury trial. None of them prohibits waiver of this right, except in capital cases. The result, however, is that only a minority of cases are actually tried by jury.

[1] Capitol Traction Co. v. Hof, 174 U.S. 1 (1899).

The right to a trial by jury is exercised in this way. In criminal cases—except those that call for the death penalty—a defendant is informed that he has the right to a jury trial and that he can elect to have a trial by jury, or that he can waive a trial by jury. No cost is charged to a defendant. In civil cases, any party may demand a trial by jury, in which event he deposits with the court a small sum of money. In both jury and non-jury trials of civil cases, court costs are charged against the losing party. In both criminal and civil cases, if a jury is not used the trial is conducted by one or more trial judges.

The courts in the United States are divided into two systems, the federal courts and the state courts. Each constitution provides what judicial power shall be vested in each court that they create.

The federal system of courts consists of District Courts, which are given power, or jurisdiction, over a specified area of all or part of a state, and Circuit Courts of Appeals (of which there are eleven) with power to hear appeals from District Courts in the states assigned to them. Then at the top is the United States Supreme Court. Jury trials are held in the District Courts only.

The state system of courts consists of courts which sit at the county seat of each county. These courts have jurisdiction over parts of a county, a whole county, or more than one county, according to the will of the legislature. Courts covering more than one county are known as Circuit Courts; they circulate, holding terms of court at each county seat. These are the trial courts. In large cities, there are courts with jurisdiction over the area of a whole city. These have various names, such as City Court, Municipal Court, Court of Special Sessions, and in them the legislatures usually provide for the same jury trial system that is used in County Courts. (There are also minor courts, such as Police Courts, and courts held by Justices of Peace. They may or may not use a jury, and the jury need not be twelve in number. We are not concerned with them.)

Appeals may be taken from these trial courts to the appellate courts. A losing litigant can make an initial appeal as a

17

matter of right. In fourteen states there are intermediate appeals courts, as in the federal system. These courts are set up to relieve the load of cases which would otherwise go to the top courts. Further appeal to the top courts is by permission under such conditions as may be set by the legislatures or permitted to be made by the courts. The three most generally permitted cases are those in which the petition seeking permission to appeal shows that a constitutional issue is involved; cases in which two intermediate courts have held differently on an issue of law, and cases which are of concern to a large segment of the public.

Appellate Courts do not take testimony. Their function is to determine matters of law, that is, to rule on errors claimed to have been committed in the trial court.

All County Courts are common law courts, so, for convenience, wherever we refer to courts which use the jury trial system we will feel free to refer to them as County Courts. This is appropriate, since in 1776 both England and the colonies used counties as governmental divisions.

We have used the word jurisdiction in the limited sense of the area over which the authority of a court extends—the area where its writs, orders, and judgments are legally effective. What does "jurisdiction" mean in terms of geography? Here is an example. Some years ago, a group of townsmen went to a secluded place in the countryside for a Saturday afternoon of sport in gambling on cock fights. The sheriff from the town and his deputies swooped down and arrested about a dozen men. Half of them went to one lawyer and were advised to plead guilty and stand being fined. This they did. The others went to another lawyer who advised them to plead not guilty, which they did. At the trial it was proved that the fights and the arrests took place at a location just over the far side of the county border. The defendants were all discharged for lack of jurisdiction, because the county court could not try people arrested for a crime committed outside the county.

Jurisdiction also applies to the nature of the crime committed.

A court has jurisdiction to try whatever crimes the legislature authorizes. Jurisdiction also applies to the amount of damages which may be awarded in civil cases. So, some courts are limited to try cases up to a certain claimed amount while other courts can award unlimited damages. If a man wishes to enforce a claim to ten thousand dollars he must sue in a court having jurisdiction to award that amount. He can sue for and recover only an amount within the jurisdiction of the court that he uses.

Jurisdiction applies also to the type of cases which a court has authority to try and to render judgment in. County Courts control all of the types of litigation which arise under the common law and litigation over similar matters created by legislation. The legislatures may delegate some of this general jurisdiction to minor magistrate courts. A magistrate's court can try cases that are triable by jury. The losing party can appeal to the County Court and, as a matter of right, have a retrial with a jury.

With fifty legislatures plus the Congress of the United States having the authority to pass legislation which affects jury trials in their courts, it would be impossible to describe the jury trial system, if it were not for the saving grace of the common law. Due to the fact that jury trials everywhere in the United States are common law trials, there is a common framework on which all jury trials are conducted. That makes it possible to broadly describe the system without explaining all the particular and, for our purposes, unimportant variations from state to state. For instance, it is of some importance to the general public that we state that the general rule in trials is that the affirmative side of a case opens and closes the argument to the jury. It is not important that in two states the right to open and close argument is with the defense, provided the defense offered no evidence; nor is it necessary that we point out every exception to the general rules.

The reader will have in mind that we write of the jury trial system on a broad basis, describing the procedure generally followed in jury trials, but avoiding the myriad exceptions which exist on relatively minor points. The old saying is that there are exceptions to every rule. That saying is nowhere more apt than in all phases of law. So, as anybody speaking of a rule does not mention all the exceptions which can be made, we will cover the rule and will not undertake to bore the reader by noting exceptions which have only local or limited application.

3

The Search for Jurors

THERE are several stages in the procedure which must be followed in the process whereby citizens become jurors. Each step is prescribed by legislation. Statutory requirements have been interpreted in two ways. Some state courts hold them to be mandatory and consequently any departure from the prescribed requirements will result in the entire panel being dismissed. In a recent case, the entire panel was dismissed because one venireman had moved from the city to the suburbs after his name had been placed in the jury box. In other state courts the requirements are held to be directory only, and only a substantial departure from the prescribed requirements is fatal. So, in the instance cited above, the venireman would be excused from duty and replaced by another. Such an offense as stuffing the jury box would be substantial and would result in the discharge of the entire panel.

Every jury trial court is required by legislation to have a few men, usually three, to act as jury commissioners. They have the duty to regularly provide the trial courts with a list of enough prospective jurors to meet the ordinary and usual requirements of the courts.

The first act of the commissioners is to compile a list of a specified number of those in the community who are eligible for jury service. The names may be obtained in various ways— from voting records, tax rolls, street directories, or other existing lists.

Statutes define the qualifications necessary for jury service. They will usually exclude those who have a criminal record, who cannot understand the English language, or who have a physical disability. They may also stipulate literacy, residence, voting, or property requirements. Here is a typical statute:

No person shall be competent to act as a juror unless he be a citizen of the United States, and a resident of the state, over twenty-one years of age and under sixty-five years of age, able to read and write and to understand the English language, and a good and lawful person, who has never been convicted of a felony or a misdemeanor involving moral turpitude.

Under the common law, women were not eligible to serve as jurors, except in one peculiar situation—cases involving feigned pregnancy. They are now eligible in most state courts and in federal courts. In some states, service is on a voluntary basis. In other states, it is compulsory. Women's organizations are trying to make women eligible in all states, and in all probability they will eventually succeed.

Other statutes list those persons who are specifically exempted from jury duty such as sheriffs, coroners, policemen, firemen, court and civic personnel, clergymen, members of the armed services, and certain professional people. These exemptions are automatic.

When the list of names of the necessary number of eligible citizens has been compiled, these names, typed on small pieces of paper, are placed in a box which is then locked, sealed, and safeguarded until just before prospective jurors are needed at the beginning of a new term of court. Although one must be eligible before his name may be placed in the box, eligibility for jury service does not *entitle* one to have his name placed in the box. And even though the names placed in the box should compose a reasonably true cross-section of the community, no specific group may demand proportionate representation. For instance, the fact that a community may be equally divided between two religious sects does not entitle either of those sects to supply half the names in the box.

However, since the law specifically prohibits any intentional or systematic exclusion of names because of race, religion, social status, occupation, earning capacity, political affiliation, or geographical location within the area involved, the simple law of averages should produce a fair representation of all interests. If such discrimination can be shown to exist, an appeal may be made by the loser of the case, under the provisions of the Fourteenth Amendment, all the way to the United States Supreme Court.

When the time comes that names are to be withdrawn from the box, the box is unlocked and the seal broken in public. Then the commissioners draw the desired number of names and again lock and seal the box and return it to a place for safekeeping. In a few states the names are drawn and placed on a wheel which is spun for each selection.

Those persons whose names have been drawn are now called veniremen. The list of names is available to anyone. The jury commissioners have no duty to consult the willingness or convenience of veniremen; all the commissioners are supposed to do is deliver to the clerk of court the list of names drawn.

Just before the term or sitting of a court starts, the veniremen are formally served with a summons to be present in court at a certain time. Any venireman who does not respond to the summons may be arrested and brought into court. There he may be fined for his failure to respond. In counties with a relatively small population the entire panel will assemble in the courtroom at the time set in the summons. In large cities several jury trials will be going on at the same time in different courtrooms. In these instances a room is usually provided for the new panel of veniremen to assemble in. The usual practice in these courts is to send a sub-panel of twenty or more veniremen to a particular courtroom just before a case is called for trial.

After a panel is in the courtroom and the judge enters and takes his place he may state that he will hear requests of veniremen to be excused from duty. In the absence of such a statement a venireman may go to the judge and state any reasons why he should be excused from service. Courts are

23

not set up to cause hardships to citizens, so if the venireman can convince the judge that service would be a hardship, the judge can excuse him from any jury duty or he may grant a delay.

Some people attempt to avoid jury service for reasons such as dread of the unknown, fear of public embarrassment at the hands of probing lawyers, or apprehension about becoming involved in a full-time, lengthy process that will seal them off from their normal pursuits.

The fear of the unknown is dangerous and should be corrected, since a free country depends upon an informed citizenry. The idea that jurors are subjected to painful grilling probably comes from press stories about days spent in questioning prospective jurors. These cases are very rare. In the vast majority of trials a jury is impanelled in twenty minutes to an hour, without publicity, and with a minimum of questioning. By the same token, the lengthy and complicated trial is relatively rare. Trials will ordinarily consume one to five court days, and there are many more short trials than long ones. Furthermore, a prospective juror may not be accepted on any jury during the term of his service, and when not actually hearing a case, he may be excused early for the day, or he may even be permitted to conduct his business from the courthouse.

A point of view held by many people is: "They have plenty of people who are willing to serve—people who are out of work, or housewives, or workers who get paid anyway. They don't need me." The answer is clear: If the jury is to represent the community as a whole, then the viewpoint of each group within it must be represented, so far as that is possible. Service may be less convenient for some than for others, but broad representation is important.

A great many people object to the inconvenience of jury service and give one reason or another why they should not serve. The only answer one can give these people is that if our particular system of law is to function, each person must accept his share of the community's responsibility for maintain-

24

ing those sacred rights guaranteed to each of us by the Constitution.

One criticism frequently leveled at the jury trial system is that it does not provide juries which represent a true cross-section of the community. To some degree, this seems to be true. Certainly, anyone who has observed a series of jury panels will have noticed how seldom the names of community leaders come out of the jury box. One rarely finds an important industrialist, labor leader, banker, businessman, or any socially prominent person among prospective jurors. In fact, it often seems that the entire upper-income group manages somehow to remove itself from jury service, probably through political, social, or economic influence. Obviously, the absence of this group does make it impossible for the typical jury panel to reflect the community as a whole.

Another frequent but far less valid criticism is that the typical juror is not competent to decide questions of fact and understand the applicable law. This criticism overlooks the essential point that, with a few exceptions to be discussed later, jurors determine the true facts of a case to the best of their ability. They essentially determine which witness tells the truth and which tells lies. Intelligence and common sense are the important attributes of a juror, and these qualities are not limited to persons of any particular background, training, or education.

Finally it may be said that those persons who seek to evade jury duty overlook the positive values in jury service. Not only will jury experience give the average citizen a valuable insight into the workings of our judicial system, but it will provide a valuable lesson on how different minds and divergent viewpoints can be brought to an acceptable group decision.

The problem of getting the right names into the jury box is being met successfully in many counties through the close cooperation of the jury commissioners, judges, lawyers, and civic leaders. However, only through an informed public, willing to accept the responsibilities of citizenship, can this problem really be solved.

In this chapter we have advanced a prospective juror from the status of a citizen to the status of a venireman, ready to be called to serve as a juror in a case which has been called for trial. A discerning reader will notice that no provision has been set forth for instructing him in his duties as a juror or in his conduct as a juror. Nor has any instruction been given to him on his rights as a juror. This absence of instruction is in conformity with common law practice and, though it may seem a bit strange, it has not been a serious detriment to the jury trial system.

A few courts now call veniremen to one or more sessions of instruction, but it is questionable whether a court has authority, in the absence of legislation so providing, to compel a venireman to attend sessions devoted to instruction or the authority to pay a venireman for time spent in attending instruction sessions.

4

The Selection of a Jury

IN the last chapter we advanced veniremen as far as the court-room. This room, laid out in much the same manner in all courthouses, is oblong in shape and is divided crosswise by a barrier. This barrier is called the bar, the same word which is used to designate lawyers collectively and spoken of as the bar of the court. In the rear of this bar, seats are provided for spectators and it is in these seats that veniremen sit when they sit as a group. At the far end of the room there is a chair and worktable for the judge. This is elevated two or three steps. This place is called the bench. The word bench originally was applied to the judges of the court, for whom a sitting bench was provided. The judges eligible to sit were spoken of as the bench of the court. Lawyers still ask, "Who is sitting on the bench today?" When, during a trial, a lawyer wishes to confer with the judge in a degree of privacy he will ask, "May we approach the bench?" He may be asking to approach the judge or the place where the judge is sitting. In front of the judge a worktable and chair are provided for the clerk of the court, and beside the judge, on one or both sides, a chair is provided for witnesses as they testify. The clerk's chair and the witness's are one step above floor level. The space in which a witness sits is spoken of as the witness stand, this being a carry-over from the days when witnesses actually did stand while giving testimony. To one side of the room is an enclosure with an opening at one end, and two rows of six or seven chairs. The front row is one step above floor level and the rear row is elevated two steps. This enclosure is spoken of as the jury box, a repetition of the word box, meaning the box from which names of veniremen were drawn.

In the remaining floor space, two tables with chairs are set up. The table nearer the jury box is provided for the side which has the positive of the case (the prosecutor or the plaintiff), and the other table is for the defense. These tables and chairs provide space for the trial lawyers and the litigants. In front of the bar, a row of chairs is provided for lawyers who have business with the judge or sit as spectators. While a judge is on the bench he has control of the people in the courtroom. He is provided with a deputy whose duty is to preserve order and to see that the judge's orders are obeyed.

The court which uses the room has definite jurisdiction or power. If it be a county court, its power or authority is limited to the area within the county lines. Its power may be limited as to the particular crimes that can be tried in the court or the amount of money that can be sued for. So, all courts and judges are limited to a designated geographical area and to designated powers so that, if at any time during the trial of a case, the evidence discloses a lack of jurisdiction, the trial will be halted and the case dismissed. Even though the litigants may prefer to continue a trial, after lack of jurisdiction has been shown, the court cannot proceed because litigants have no authority to confer jurisdiction on the court.

The first step in a trial is to satisfy any doubt that the statutory procedure has been followed up to this point. If a doubt exists, the lawyer who raises the question may challenge the jury panel. This challenge is spoken of as challenge to the array. If this challenge is allowed, the panel is dismissed, but it is unusual for this to happen. (This challenge to the array has been the basis on which the legality of a jury list which did not contain the names of Negroes has been tested under the Fourteenth Amendment in the United States Supreme Court some twenty-five times since the year 1879.)

The panel must now stand examination as to the fitness of each member to serve. This examination is called the *voir dire,* which means an oath taken to tell the truth. In about two-thirds of the states this examination is under oath.

The purpose of this examination is to assure that only quali-

28

fied, unbiased, and unprejudiced jurors sit in the trial. If this purpose is accomplished, the trial can start with a reasonable expectation that the jury will render a fair and true verdict.

It is the duty of the judge to carry out this purpose. The duty never shifts to any other person, nor is there legislation in any state which eases the judge's responsibility. The manner in which he performs this duty must of necessity be left to his sound discretion. It is not left to his mere discretion, but to his *sound* discretion. Therefore, his exercise of discretion may be tested in a higher court which will rule whether his exercise of discretion was sound. The many tests which have been made have established certain standards of discretion. Judges act on the basis of these standards. There is, therefore, a degree of uniformity in the application of judicial discretion.

The judge may, and in many courts does, conduct the *voir dire,* to the exclusion of direct questioning of the panel by lawyers in the case. (Three states expressly give the lawyers this right in felony cases, and two states give the right in civil cases.) In no court, however, may the lawyers be barred from participation in some manner. Whenever the judge conducts the *voir dire,* he must give the lawyers an opportunity to participate. He will do so by accepting questions, sometimes written and sometimes oral, and, if the questions are proper, will propound them to the panel; or he will permit the lawyers to question the panel and, indeed, to conduct the entire *voir dire,* but always under his supervision.

On the other hand, in a great many courts, the lawyers customarily conduct the *voir dire.* The names of the veniremen have been made public and therefore are available to lawyers and litigants. In most courts, a typed list of the names of the veniremen who compose the panel is provided, and, in some states, the names of veniremen who will sit in a criminal trial must be supplied to the defendant's lawyer before the trial. The judge has the authority to limit the lawyers strictly to questions which may bring out causes for challenge. At times a rather fine line is drawn, such as was done in this case. A boy was pumping a small wagon diagonally across a street in the middle of the block. He was struck by an automobile operated by an off-duty fireman whose job was to drive a hose wagon. The panel was asked whether the fact that the defendant drove a hose wagon would influence any of them. This question seemed proper as some member of the panel might have a fixed opinion that because the defendant drove the wagon to fires he might be prone to drive fast at other times. The judge interrupted to say: "Don't answer that question." He then explained that he did not think the question was proper because it inferred that the members of the panel would violate their oath.

In areas where the population is relatively small and rather stable, it is not too difficult for lawyers to gather enough information about each venireman to enable them to frame questions about his qualifications. Therefore, no extended examination is necessary, and the restricted *voir dire* is workable. However, in cities few litigants have the money to pay the large expense of investigation and consequently all information must be secured through the *voir dire*. An extended examination may be necessary and this may be conducted more effectively by the lawyers.

Another circumstance is the importance of the trial. In a simple case, the restrictive method is generally satisfactory. In other cases, such as felony, libel and, malpractice, so much is at stake—by way of liberty, money and reputation—that extended examination by the lawyers seems preferable.

It is in these cases of large importance to the litigants that the power of money first comes into play. If a lawyer is supplied with an abundance of money he can make a detailed investigation of every venireman on the list. He can learn their moral and ethical standards and their financial circumstances. He can learn their moral attitudes. He may even learn of actual statements made by a venireman which will disqualify him. This advantage of financial status of one litigant over the other cannot be controlled by the court. But it can be mitigated somewhat by allowing extensive *voir dire*.

The third circumstance is the reaction of the litigants and the public. There should be no basis for a claim by a litigant that

30

the examination was not permitted to be sufficiently broad in scope to bring out all the facts. Necessary time should be allowed to satisfy litigants of the fitness of each venireman. Extended examination may seem inefficient and time-consuming, but the jury system is not designed for efficiency. It is designed to be a system which is acceptable to and approved by the citizens.

In the *voir dire,* the veniremen are first given a brief description of the nature of the case, and the litigants are identified. Then questions are asked in an attempt to reveal the legal qualification of each venireman. In some courts, the examination takes place as the panel sits as a unit; in other courts, the jury box is filled with veniremen and members are replaced as may be required. If any juror is shown to be unqualified he is challenged and excused from further participation in the trial. This is called challenge for cause.

Next, the venireman is subject to challenge if any of these facts, among others, appears: He has a pecuniary interest in the outcome of the trial; he is a stockholder in a corporation involved in the trial; he is related to someone involved in the trial; he benefited or was injured by the crime or act; he has a fixed opinion of merit, guilt, or innocence; he has an opinion based on what was told to him by one having personal knowledge and would be influenced thereby; he has an opinion of the law of the case which he would honor above judicial instruction; he has an opinion that a particular act is not wrong or a crime and will not change his opinion; he is opposed to the prospective punishment and will not consider available alternates; he has scruples against the death penalty; he will not apply the presumption of innocence, or he will not convict on circumstantial evidence.

Whenever the answers received indicate apparent or possible unfitness, the lawyer may voice a challenge. Each such challenge is, in fact, litigation involving law, fact, or both, and is decided under the discretionary power of the judge. If the challenge is upheld the venireman is excused from the trial.

In the course of this examination no venireman may be made

to answer a question which will bring disgrace, infamy, or self-accusation of crime. Questions not pertinent are not proper. Should a venireman be in doubt whether he need answer a question, he can withhold his answer until the judge rules on the propriety of the question. The judge will not interfere in the examination except when a lawyer obviously abuses his right or privilege to examine.

The most common cause for disqualification is the presence of bias or prejudice. The words "bias" and "prejudice" are used relatively because all men are biased or prejudiced in some respects. Men deny being biased or prejudiced, since the words have ....n on connotations which make them derogatory. So, if veniremen are asked singly or collectively if any are biased or prejudiced there will be no affirmative response. Disclosure must be brought out indirectly.

These two words are of such importance that a clear understanding should exist as to the mental processes involved. They are, therefore, defined.

Bias is properly used to express the idea that incoming impressions are slanted off so that the impressions do not follow direct paths in the mind. For example, derogatory comments on the acts of members of a person's family or close friends are shunted into the area of excuse. There they lose their impact. We are *biased* towards family and friends.

Prejudice is properly used to express the idea that a mental block exists against incoming ideas which conflict with fixed ideas. We note prejudice in mothers of wayward children who know that the children are wayward but refuse to allow the truth to enter into their minds. So, derogatory remarks regarding their children have no effect. This is *prejudice* in favor of children.

If bias or prejudice is brought out, the further question must be asked whether the disclosed attitude would affect the venireman in reaching a verdict. If so, the venireman is subject to disqualification for cause. Disqualification is not based on the presence of bias or prejudice. It is based on obstinate attachment to personal opinions. (It would be proper to speak of this state of mind as *bigoted*.)

Now the panel is reduced in number to veniremen who have qualified as being disinterested and fair-minded. Usually, the number is more than sufficient to compose a jury. These veniremen are subject to one more challenge, for which no reason is, or need be, stated. This challenge is called peremptory (absolute). The number of peremptory challenges in a civil trial may be up to four, and in criminal trials may be up to twenty, depending on the location of the trial.

Peremptory challenges in minor trials are more or less perfunctory and are used chiefly to reduce the panel to the required number of jurors. In important trials they give lawyers an opportunity to exercise their judgment as to the desirability or undesirability of individual veniremen. Every lawyer naturally wants to weed out veniremen who would be unfavorable to the lawyer's cause.

There is no conflict between the aim of the law to secure qualified and unbiased jurors and the aim of lawyers to secure a favorable jury. Lawyers are free to use their preconceived notions of the probable bias of groups and individuals. Consequently, few juries are selected without consideration of possible benefit or harm from striking or failing to strike members of the panel on the basis of age, mentality, sex, race, nationality, economic status, education, and occupation. There is a general impression among lawyers that male jurors, out of gallantry, favor women litigants and so, when representing a woman, they seek an all-male jury which will overlook female deceit another woman would spot at once. There is an impression that a jury will favor a litigant of his own race or creed. With the right to strike four members from the panel, it is generally possible to strike all members of a sex or race, but it is hard to strike all of both.

An instance will illustrate this: In an automobile accident at an intersection, a white woman passenger in one car claimed that she suffered a sprain at the sacroiliac joint and sustained

33

pleurisy, through the negligence of the driver of the other car, a Negro. Her attorney sought a settlement out of court. When that was refused, he said that he would get an all-white jury and that an all-white jury would give his client a large verdict. At the trial he did get an all-white jury, but he also got two women jurors. The foreman of the jury reported a finding for the woman. When the clerk of court asked in what amount, the foreman answered in the amount of one dollar. It appeared that he had stage fright and had meant to say one thousand dollars. But he was asked to repeat the amount of the award and again said one dollar.

The foreman of the jury later reported that, when the jurors began their deliberations, he had asked them to write on a slip of paper what amount, if any, they would award the plaintiff. One of the women spoke up and, waving aside the piece of paper, said that she was a nurse, that the plaintiff was a faker, and that she would award one dollar and no more. Then the other woman juror spoke up and said she also would award only one dollar. The foreman said that the men argued with the women for an hour and a half but the women would not budge from one dollar, and the men had to finally agree with them.

Lawyers evaluate veniremen on the information about them which has been acquired from pretrial investigation, from observing them about the courthouse and in previous trials, and from observing them during the *voir dire*. During the *voir dire* the veniremen may be required to identify themselves, perhaps by standing, and they are required to speak in answer to questions. The wise use of the information so gathered may mean the difference between a case won and a case lost.

In everyday life, when we meet a stranger we evaluate him; we size him up. We get an impression that we will like him, be neutral, or be lacking in harmony with him. Our future relations are affected by this evaluation. The evaluation is much more important in litigation.

A lawyer may rely on his natural ability to size up people, taking an interest in items of appearance which are beyond

34

what he regards as normal. Or a lawyer may make a study of physiognomy or phrenology. These pursuits are not accepted as sciences by all people, but the fact that one book[1] on the subject sold over 600,000 copies is evidence of general interest. The author does not pose as an authority on these subjects and will go no further than to briefly summarize some of the characteristics, which, according to Belkin's book, are indicated by certain physical features. Some of these are: Eyebrows meet and eyes are close together—narrow-mindedness. Narrowly closed eyelids—deceit. Upper lid covering more than a third of iris—secretiveness. Round, wide eyes—credulousness. Large round eyes—perception. Small eyes—short on emotion. Downcast eyes—timidity and over-caution. Pointed ears with no lobes—dishonesty. Flat-topped ears—tight with money. Short upper lip—sensitiveness, fears criticism, loves praise and flattery, responds to charm. Long upper lip—individualist, impervious to flattery, responds to logic. Drooping corners of mouth—pessimism. Upturned corners of mouth—optimism. Wide mouth—generosity. Full lips—emotional.

Another applicable study is anthropometry, which is based on the physical aspects of the human body. This study divides people into three classifications. *Endomorphs* are round and soft of body, have wide faces, short necks and tend to be obese. They have bland faces, are deliberate of speech, even-tempered and relaxed. They are amiable. These qualities make them more generous to criminal defendants and civil plaintiffs. *Mesomorphs* have square, athletic-type bodies, strong voices, and seem to be older than their age. They give particular attention to facts. They are, therefore, for the side which has a strong factual basis. *Ectomorphs* are lean, underweight, and have fragile features. They have weak voices and an appearance of intentness and strain. They are least amiable and generous. These qualities make them less generous to criminal defendants and civil plaintiffs.

Observant persons realize that their judgment of a person is

[1] *How to Measure Your Power,* by H. H. Belkin (Halcyon House, 1938).

instinctively in accord with these characteristics, whenever a person fits predominately into any of the classifications stated. But physiognomy, phrenology, and anthropometry receive no support from geneticists. These authorities hold that there is no set relationship between the genes which produce body structures and the genes which produce mental characteristics. Therefore, they hold that whenever a relationship appears it is accidental.

It may seem a bit far-fetched to give consideration to physiognomy, phrenology, and anthropometry, but such is not the case. When we speak of securing favorable jurors, it is commonly understood that choice is mainly based on possible bias. That is true very often, but it is advantageous to go deeper and learn what sort of man the venireman really is. We have no dispute that men of repulsive ugliness, men obviously deformed, and men extremely tall or short tend to develop resentments. We can accept the fact that these men acquire peculiar mental attitudes, because we can see a cause. We associate a type of mind with what we see. Is it then not reasonable to assume that physical characteristics reflect type of mentality as well as types of emotional response? Those lawyers who accept these physical factors as valid will use them to get jurors of the type of mind most desired in the light of the facts expected to be proved in the particular case at trial.

The author knows of no scientific study to determine whether physiology can be used to determine the attitudes of different types of people toward liability or guilt. However, in a recent survey of the amount of award in civil cases favored by ex-jurors, it was found that people who tire themselves out in attempting to do too much (probably ectomorphs) favored average money awards about thirty-seven per cent of the average amount favored by the other ex-jurors in the survey. In other words, the ectomorphic jurors would award $370 where the others would award $1,000.

This survey did determine that type of employment had a definite bearing on the amount of damages jurors allowed in civil cases, indicating a wide variation in the value placed on money. Taking the average awards of damages favored by the proprietor and professional classes as 100 per cent, the survey showed that the clerical class average was 112.9 per cent, skilled workers 122.6 per cent and unskilled workers 145.1 per cent.

Veniremen who have not been selected for the jury have no reason to feel hurt, slighted, or rejected. The reason may have been that they appeared undesirably intelligent, unduly wise in human nature, or too smart to be beguiled. The fact is that a venireman seldom has any basis for knowing why he was not selected to sit. We have followed custom in speaking of *selecting* a jury, when, in fact, we do the opposite. We *reject* veniremen, and those who are not rejected form the jury.

The number of veniremen challenged and excused, or stricken by peremptory challenge, may reduce the panel to a number insufficient to complete a jury. If this happens, other names may be drawn from the jury box and summoned into court, or the sheriff may summon bystanders or persons nearby. These persons whose names were not in the jury box are designated as talesmen (called men). These new people must stand the same qualification and fitness tests as the veniremen who preceded them.

It is not unusual to select one or two alternate jurors who sit in the case and are ready to substitute for any juror who becomes unable to continue because of illness or other reasons.

The *voir dire* having ended, the veniremen who have been accepted are sworn in as jurors, and the trial proceeds. A comment may be made that up to this time the veniremen (now the jurors) have not seen the witnesses nor heard any evidence. Thus at best, they have answered questions which revealed their states of mind at that moment, but there is no assurance that by the end of the trial they will not be biased or prejudiced —perhaps even bigoted. Nor is there assurance that a venireman who was biased and is biased toward one party, and yet escaped disqualification, will not reverse his attitude before the verdict is rendered.

The unpredictability of change of attitude by jurors between

37

the beginning and the end of a trial gives support to those who question the value of *voir dire*. At the same time, it shows the advantage of judging veniremen by obvious physical chacacteristics.

A few words need to be said about *special juries* because the public can become confused when juries are spoken of as such. Special juries were used at the common law when the issues at trial promised to be too complex to be fairly tried by the less intelligent veniremen (issues expressed at the common law as of "too great nicety"). A special jury's members are chosen from the list of veniremen in some special manner or veniremen are rejected in some special manner. The conduct of the trial is not affected.

The common form of special jury is called a struck jury. Such a jury can be formed in several ways. One way is to supply the lawyers with the names of a specified even number of names of veniremen. Then each party strikes the same number of names to reduce the number to twelve. Another way is to assemble a panel of qualified veniremen and allow each party to strike a name alternately until the panel is reduced to twelve. Still another way is to allow the lawyers to notify the clerk of the court that the names of certain veniremen, in number set by statute, are to be striken from the panel of veniremen supplied for this particular trial. Those stricken are still held available for other trials.

The special jury in New York State, which has received wide publicity, is spoken of as the Blue Ribbon Jury. This jury is available in important criminal cases and those cases which have been greatly publicized before trial. The members of the panel come from the regular jury list but go through a preliminary examination under the supervision of the clerk, who weeds out those disqualified to serve: those with a record of crime or fraud; those against the death penalty; those against enforcement of the particular crime involved; those who will not convict on circumstantial evidence or for a particular offense; those who will not give the accused the benefit of the presumption of innocence if the defendant does not testify; and those whose verdict would be swayed by newspaper accounts which they have read or information which they have acquired.

The veniremen who have been selected as jurors then are assembled in the jury box and take a juror's oath. The oath is in a form which binds the conscience of the juror. This oath is mandatory in criminal cases but in some states it can be waived in civil trials. The oath may be given in each separate trial, and usually is, or it may be given for the term of court.

The obligation of this oath may vary in wording from state to state, but the success—and even the preservation of trial by jury—depends upon the jurors' performing according to this oath. The oath will include the obligations "well and truly to try the case" and "a true verdict render."

The obligation "well and truly to try the case" requires strict attention to the facts as they are brought out, and continuous observation of witnesses to determine what value should be given to the testimony of each witness by the ability to remember the facts; the ability of the witness to put his thoughts into words; his background and training; his interest in the outcome of the trial; any vindictiveness or any motive making him alter, shade, or vary the truth; and other observations affecting the worth of his testimony.

The obligation to render "a true verdict" means that after the case is given over to the jury for decision, jurors will diligently try to determine the truth as it may be pieced together from conflicting testimony; that they will discuss the facts with fellow jurors with an open mind; and that they will not permit emotions to sway their efforts to determine the facts and reach a verdict. They will not allow prejudice, against any person, corporation, or organization to color their mental processes as they attempt to reach a verdict.

The ancient form of a juror's oath has been continued in use, but the attitude toward the oath has changed. When oaths were first used, people believed that punishment would follow a violation—a punishment inflicted by or through the power to which the oath was addressed. That concept is obsolete. The oath in this day is an affirmation of a moral duty. The force of

39

the oath is dependent upon the moral fiber of the individual. The larger part of the value of the juror's oath is that jurors individually and collectively take upon themselves a formal moral obligation to the litigants and to each other, to honorably perform their duty to the best of their ability. It is safe to state that the vast majority of jurors take this oath with a sincere intent to abide by it.

In spite of the *voir dire,* and especially when the veniremen are examined as a panel rather than individually, some people are selected for jurors who should not sit. This can come about by inadvertence or by design. The *voir dire* will not convert a man who is without honor into a man of honor. Nor will the oath prevent a man of honor from continuing to be a man of honor. The following actual incidents are right in point: In one case, after a trial had proceeded for about fifteen minutes with the plaintiff on the stand, the courtroom door opened and a large man entered the room, took a measured look around and departed. Then a juror raised his hand and when the judge turned to him the juror asked if the man who had just come into the room was related to the plaintiff, as they had the same name. The plaintiff answered that the man was her husband. The juror then said that he had not connected the husband and wife by their last names, that he did not know her, but that he was a very good friend of her husband's and, therefore, he thought his relationship might sway his verdict. He was excused and trial continued, by consent, with eleven jurors.

In contrast to the honesty of this juror consider another actual case. The plaintiff, a merchant, had filed a claim with his insurance company for merchandise claimed to have been stolen. The company would not pay because of suspicious circumstances, so the merchant sued the company. The merchant lost the case. After the jury was discharged one juror approached the lawyer for the defendant. The juror said that he had a store near that of the merchant, that the merchant was the biggest crook on the Avenue, and that he would not believe a word the merchant said, oath or no oath. Apparently, this man got on this jury just to do what he could to see that the merchant did not win the case.

5

Criminal—or Civil?

It has already been brought out that there are two types of cases: criminal actions and civil actions. Juries function in both types of cases. The trial of either type of case, whether it be by judge or jury, will follow the steps described in the following pages.

The essential requirement in all trials is that the trial be by "due process of law." This term "due process of law" appears in the Fifth Amendment to the Constitution of the United States, which provides that no person shall "be deprived of life, liberty, or property without due process of law." In 1964, the United States Supreme Court held that this amendment applied in federal and state courts. This amendment, therefore, is a limitation in all courts. The same term also appears in the Fourteenth Amendment, Section I, which prohibits any state from depriving any person "of life, liberty or property without due process of law." It is thereby made applicable on a nationwide basis.

The principle of due process is inherited from England and goes back to Magna Charta. It was embodied in many state constitutions before the Fourteenth Amendment became effective in 1868. The term "due process of law" can be defined as notice and opportunity to be heard in orderly proceedings adapted to the nature of the case before a tribunal having jurisdiction of the cause. The term demands that laws and procedure shall not be unreasonable, arbitrary, or capricious, and the means selected for trial shall have a substantial relationship to the object sought to be attained. As applied to jury trials, due process means that before a man's life, liberty, and property may be taken he must be given notice of the proceedings which

41

may terminate in the taking, and be given an opportunity to be heard in his own defense. He must have a fair and impartial trial according to the prescribed form of judicial procedure existing where he is tried. He has a right to be represented by a lawyer and, if a person has accused him, he must have the right to face his accuser.

People in the United States have the safeguarding of this principle of due process as a priceless heritage. The principle is fully satisfied by the trial systems in effect in jury trials.

The two types of cases will be considered separately so as to bring out the peculiar aspects of each and to point out the differences in the situations of the parties involved.

Criminal trials involve crime. What is crime? It is a wrong directly affecting the public, to which the state has annexed certain punishments and penalties and which it prosecutes in its own name in a criminal proceeding. It may also be defined as an act or omission which is prohibited by law because it is injurious to the public.

Crimes may be classified in several ways. One classification divides crime into two groups. One group is designated as *mala in se,* that is, acts which are immoral or wrong in themselves, such as murder, rape, arson, burglary, larceny, or forgery. These acts have been crimes all through history and so became crimes in the United States. These crimes, being historic, have remained stable, but they have broadened to cover aspects of a crime which arise in a complex society. So, by legislation, we have murder in the first and second degree and, in addition, manslaughter and death by wrongful act. By legislation we have divided larceny into grand larceny, petty larceny, and larceny after trust.

The other group of crimes in this classification is designated as *mala prohibita,* that is, acts which are prohibited because they infringe on the rights of other persons and are crimes only because the acts are prohibited by statute. These crimes are added to endlessly as density of population increases. For instance, a person had a right to expectorate anywhere, although such act may be contrary to good manners. In a sparsely populated area such an act does no harm. When, however, people congregate in theatres such an act is harmful to the audience. The law-making body takes notice of the health hazard and prohibits it by law. These crimes created by statute include health laws, fire-escape laws, air pollution-control laws, prohibition of gambling devices in public places, postal laws, price discrimination, and violation of regulations promulgated by such agencies as the Securities and Exchange Commission.

Another broad division of crimes is into two groups called felonies and misdemeanors. Those acts just mentioned as crimes *mala in se* are called felonies. These are the serious crimes which call for the death penalty or imprisonment in federal or state prisons. Misdemeanors are offenses lesser in grade than felonies and call for punishment by fines or commitment to a jail. Misdemeanors may also be divided into those akin to felony, such as operating an automobile while intoxicated, and less serious acts called petty misdemeanors such as blocking a sidewalk.

Then there is a designation of some crimes as crimes involving moral turpitude, which is an act contrary to justice, honesty, modesty, or good morals. This classification of crime is that which employers and social organizations are interested in. Application forms include the question whether the applicant has ever been convicted of a crime involving moral turpitude and if the answer is yes the application will likely be denied. The employer desires to screen out people who are, or who may become, dishonest, as indicated by past records.

There is still another designation—that of infamous crime. The Fifth Amendment requires that such crimes prosecuted in federal courts must be on an indictment of a grand jury.

A grand jury is a body of men, in number twelve to twenty-three, summoned, usually from the regular jury list, for the purpose of investigating into crime in general, or acts of crime committed by individuals. It has no relation to a trial jury. The prosecuting attorney presents evidence involving crimes, for which arrests have been made or probably should be made, to the grand jury to determine if there is probable cause to hold a person or persons for trial and if so to return an indictment which sets forth the crimes for which the person is to be tried. The sessions are held in secret and are rather informal. This procedure, which can be regarded as a preliminary investigation, is a protection against unfounded prosecution. A grand jury may also investigate into any criminal situation if called upon to do so by the judge or the prosecutor. It can also initiate investigation.

The initial common law juries investigated crimes and conducted the trial of accused persons. Later, sometime after the Norman invasion, the functions of the jury were divided. The determination of probable cause for bringing a culprit to trial was delegated to a separate body designated a *grand jury*. The ensuring trial was then held by a trial jury designated a *petit jury*.

A state may *authorize* infamous crimes to be prosecuted by "an information"—the filing of an official charge without the necessity of obtaining a grand jury indictment. Whether a crime is infamous depends upon the punishment the court has power to inflict and not upon the nature of the crime. Infamous crimes include those where the punishment may be death, imprisonment in a federal prison or penitentiary, or imprisonment in a state prison with or without imposition of hard labor.

One criminal transaction may involve several different offenses, each calling for a separate charge in the indictment or information. Thus, a man arrested in a narcotics investigation may be charged with both possession of and sale of narcotics; and a man arrested for fraud may be charged with taking money by fraud from several persons at the same time. After committing *one* criminal act, a man may be charged with *several* distinct crimes.

It is difficult to classify criminal acts as felonies or misdemeanors on a nationwide basis because their classification may be determinable by each state legislature and by the Congress. So, it is apparent that a crime may be classed as a felony in one jurisdiction and as a misdemeanor in another because of the difference in legislation.

No general statement can be made as to which crimes are triable by a jury, other than that usually felonies are triable by a jury. The federal and state constitutions and statutes must be examined as they determine the right to trial by jury. This seems to be in contradiction of Article Three of the Federal Constitution and of state constitutions which contain a similar provision regarding jury trials. If, as specified in Article Three, "The trial of all crimes . . . shall be by jury," how is it that all crimes, as previously defined, are not tried by jury? The answer is found in the events of the Constitutional Convention. The draft of the Constitution, which was made by the committee of five delegates, reads: "The trial of all criminal offenses . . . shall be by jury." The delegates to the convention, having in mind that Blackstone classified all public offenses as crimes, unanimously voted that this provision should read "The trial of all crimes." This action showed a clear intent to restrict trial by jury to major crimes. This intent must be recognized as the authority for the exemption of minor crimes from jury trial. One can imagine the burden which would have been imposed on federal trial courts had this change not been made.

The appearance of the accused in court is the result of preliminary procedural actions as prescribed by the legislatures. In cases of felonies, a grand jury usually has heard testimony and found probable cause to believe that the crime charged had been committed by the defendant. Exceptions exist in that some state constitutions do not guarantee grand jury action. The state legislature can authorize both felonies and indictments to be prosecuted upon "informations." In misdemeanor cases, a complaint or accusation was heard by an authorized person who found probable cause and issued an information to hold the defendant for trial. An information is a written account of the episode prepared by the state. The defendant has vocally denied his guilt before a designated official, and has thereby raised an issue of fact which the jury will determine in a trial.

Civil trials involve claims for money or tangible property and result in verdicts awarding or denying money or property. They are commenced by one or more individuals, called plaintiffs, who assert in a written document, called a complaint, that damages are due to them from one or more individuals, called defendants. Civil actions are divided into two classifications, contract and tort.

Contract actions are based on the claim that a contract, either written or oral, has been breached by the defendant and, as a result, the plaintiff has suffered damage in the amount stated in the complaint. Some contracts are expressed in writing, such as contracts to purchase a house, which state what the owner is to convey, the amount which the purchaser will pay, and the terms of payment. Some contracts are oral. Other contracts are implied. When, for example, a person orders articles of merchandise from a store, it is implied that he has contracted to pay the sale price set by the store.

In some cases, it is relatively simple to establish the obligation to make payment and the amount of payment which should be made. In a case based, say, on a fire insurance policy, the jury task is not so simple. The jury must determine whether the insurance policy, or contract, covers the fire loss, and it must determine the amount of the loss in dollars and cents. The insurance policy may be complex, and, if the house is an old one, it is difficult to determine the amount of the loss, which is the difference in value of the house before and after the fire.

A tort is a private wrong in that it is an infringement of the rights of an individual. Tort actions are based on a claim that the defendant has breached a duty which he owes to the plaintiff and, as a result, the plaintiff has suffered damage. For example, in an automobile accident, the tort may be the breach of a duty to obey a traffic regulation. (This tort is also a misdemeanor. Thus, a single act can be the source of both a criminal prosecution and a civil action.)

A court action is commenced by the aggrieved party filing his claim in the form of a complaint. This is a voluntary act. It is also a personal act in which the state has no interest. In former days complaints were required to be precise and had to strictly conform to particular patterns according to the nature of the claim; otherwise, the case was dismissed. The unfairness

46

of having a valid claim thrown out of court because the plaintiff's lawyer erred in the wording of the complaint came to be realized. So strictness was relaxed. Today, great liberality in presentation is allowed, but it is essential that the presentation make clear to the defendant the basis of the claim; the time it arose; the nature of the damage; and the amount of damages claimed. The defendant then files a reply asserting his defense; he may also add any counter-claim he may have against the plaintiff, or any partial satisfaction already paid. The plaintiff then files an answer to any claim which defendant has asserted against him. These papers are called pleadings.

Where additional individuals have the same claim, they may be permitted to sue together. Likewise, if the claim is against several parties, who may be jointly or individually liable, they may be joined as defendants in the suit. If the claim involves other individuals in the liability asserted, these persons may be brought in as added parties, provided the court has jurisdiction over the claim. In this way the rights and duties of all parties may be disposed of in a single trial.

The amount of damages claimed in a contract case can be estimated by both the plaintiff and the defendant on a mathematical basis, so, allowing for a bit of exaggeration, the amount claimed will have a fairly close relationship to the amount which the plaintiff expects to be able to prove.

In a tort action a jury must determine whether the tort was committed by one or more persons named as a defendant, and, if one or more are proven to be at fault and therefore liable for the damage, the jury must bring in a verdict which will fairly compensate the plaintiff for the damage which he has suffered. So, if a repairman causes an explosion in an old house the same difficulty in determining the money value of the damage is encountered by the jury as was noted in the earlier example about the fire insurance case. The determination of damages is most difficult in cases involving slander, libel, and personal injury which results in suffering. This is so because there is no yardstick or guide, and because of the difference in valuation each juror puts on the dollar.

Then there is a type of damage called punitive damage which a jury can award in some cases by way of punishment. The most frequent award of punitive damage is in cases of libel and slander. In awarding punitive damage the jury is again without a yardstick.

Since the cost of filing suit for a large amount is little, if any, more than the cost of suing for a small amount, the temptation is to ask for a large amount. Asking for a large amount sometimes frightens the defendant into making a settlement which he otherwise would not make.

The filing of a complaint which asserts a claim properly pleaded is not evidence that the plaintiff has a valid claim. In fact, it may have only a nuisance value; that is, the defendant, after estimating the expense of defense, may offer to pay a small amount just to be rid of the case.

In one instance, two plaintiffs sued for $100,000 each. The judge called the lawyers to the bench and asked the defendant's lawyer if he had made any offer of settlement. The answer was no. The judge asked why not. The defendant's lawyer replied that any offer he made would be so low that the plaintiffs would not accept. The judge asked what the offer would be. The defendant's lawyer said, "One hundred dollars to each plaintiff." The judge then asked the plaintiffs' lawyer if he would accept. Surprisingly, the answer was yes.

A plaintiff cannot be successfully sued for damages because he, in good faith, filed a complaint and failed to secure a jury verdict. This is for the sound reason that a person who desires to file a suit should not be subject to penalty, and should not fear reprisal. The only penalty to a plaintiff who sues and loses is that a judgment is entered for the court costs paid by the defendant. If, however, as sometimes happens, a plaintiff who has lost his case files a second action based on the same facts that were involved in the first action, he is subject to a cross-action for malicious prosecution.

There are several major differences between criminal trials and civil trials.

In a criminal trial, the prosecutor is limited to the specific

48

charges contained in the indictment. The defendant cannot be tried for any offense not spelled out in the indictment or information. If the correct offense is not spelled out, the defendant is discharged, but is possibly subject to a re-indictment in proper wording. In a civil case, the pleadings are not so binding on the litigants; they do not lose their day in court because of a faulty pleading. The pleadings can be amended to correct any error.

The prosecutor in a criminal trial has the burden of proof to establish each and every element of the indictment or information beyond a reasonable doubt. It is not sufficient that the evidence makes jurors conclude, as a matter of opinion only, that the defendant is guilty. There must be evidence which eradicates all reasonable doubt of guilt.

The meaning of the words "reasonable doubt" has been the source of innumerable decisions, handed down because defendants' lawyers frequently seek release of their convicted clients on the basis of erroneous definitions of reasonable doubt given by the trial judge, or on the plea that the evidence raised a reasonable doubt which the jury ignored. It seems extraordinary that these two words should be the subject of so much ado. The appellate courts of at least ten states have held that the words are self-explanatory and that a jury needs no definition from the trial judge. In at least one state, the meaning of the words is set forth in a statute, and the judge need do no more than read the statute. Jurors know the meaning of "doubt" and they know the meaning of "reasonable." It therefore seems strange even to assume that they do not know the meaning of the words when joined together. Here is a summary of definitions given by the courts as to what are and are not elements of reasonable doubt: Reasonable doubt does not mean a conjecture, a speculation, a suspicion, a possibility, slightest doubt, a doubt, any doubt; nor does it mean beyond all or any doubt. On the positive side, reasonable doubt means a doubt based on reason; an honest doubt such as an upright man might entertain after honest investigation after truth; an abiding conviction to a moral certainty; or a doubt which leaves the mind of a juror wavering. Reasonable doubt must be based on all the evidence or the want of evidence.

In a civil case, the plaintiff's burden of proof is to establish his case by a fair preponderance of the evidence. To make this clear the simile of a balance scale is applicable. At the end of the trial if the credible evidence in favor of the plaintiff (plus proper inferences from the evidence) is weighed on one end of the scale against the credible evidence in favor of the defendant (plus proper inferences) on the other end, the scale must dip downward on the plaintiff's end if he is to receive a verdict in his favor. If the scale stays in balance, or if it dips downward on the defendant's end, the plaintiff must lose.

It will be noticed from these comments that a verdict of "not guilty" would be more accurate if it were in the form of "not *proven to be* guilty of the specified charge." An accused cannot secure a verdict that he is in fact not guilty. A verdict of a jury "for the defendant" in a civil case would be more accurate if in the form of "liability of the defendant *not proven*." A defendant cannot secure a verdict which in fact determines that he did not breach a contract. A verdict for the defendant goes no further than to decide that the affirmative side did not carry its burden of proof. It merely absolves the defendant.

Another difference between the two types of cases involves the manner of disposing of the cases before trial or before a verdict. A criminal case can be terminated by the prosecutor dropping the charges. This is done by making a proper entry in the record. Or, the case can be terminated by the defendant putting himself at the mercy of the judge. He does this by a plea called *nolo contendere,* which means that he does not contest the charge. A civil case can be terminated at any time by the plaintiff dismissing his complaint, and the defendant dismissing any counter-claim or cross-claim.

Yet another difference is that there is no time limit placed on bringing a suspected murderer or traitor to trial. Regardless of the lapse of time between the committing of the crime and the apprehension of the accused, he is subject to trial. Lapse of time helps him only if witnesses for the prosecution have disappeared or have died. On the other hand, every civil action is subject to a statute which specifies a time limit within which a plaintiff must file his complaint with the court. Any suit brought after the expiration of the time limit will be dismissed at the request of the defendant. The civil defendant is thus freed from liability for damages by lapse of time.

The last difference to be noted here relates to end results. An accused in a criminal trial, if found guilty, will receive an appropriate penalty. If the penalty is a fine which the accused cannot pay he will go to jail and work off the fine. A civil defendant against whom a jury renders a verdict will have a judgment entered against him. He may then evade payment and the plaintiff must make what collection he can by way of garnishment of defendant's earnings or he must locate assets belonging to the defendant and gain possession of them. The defendant may go into bankruptcy and thereby avoid payment. In the end, the plaintiff may get nothing and wind up with a loss of what he paid to prosecute his suit.

The American colonists followed the English practice of putting judgment debtors in jail. This practice was anything but popular. In 1817, states began to limit the practice to a minimum debt of about twenty-five dollars. Kentucky abolished the practice in 1821, and other states followed suit, so that within thirty years the practice was abolished in almost all states. Now the practice has returned in a new guise. In some states, including Iowa, Kansas, Massachusetts, and New York, statutes provide that a judgment debtor against whom an execution on a judgment has been returned unsatisfied can be brought into court and be examined as to his financial position. He can then be ordered to pay the judgment in a lump sum or in installments according to his ability. If he does not obey the order he is brought into court again, and, if he has no acceptable excuse, he can be sentenced to jail. These statutes have been held to be constitutional on the ground that anyone who fails to obey a court order is in contempt of court. The debtor is put in jail, not because of nonpayment of debt but because of contempt of court.

What is regarded by many people as another difference is that, in a criminal case, the accused is entitled to have the judge instruct the jury that the accused is presumed to be innocent; and that he is not guilty until proven to be guilty. As a matter of fact, in a civil case the defendant is entitled to a similar instruction from the judge: that the defendant is not liable unless his liability be proven by a preponderance of the evidence. This instruction might just as aptly be stated thus: the defendant is presumed to be not liable (innocent) until proven to be liable. An accused can remain inactive and secure until the state has established a prima facie case, but so can a civil defendant rest secure. Looked at in this way, it is obvious that inclusion of the presumption of innocence appears to be superfluous. Yet it does serve a purpose.

In the early days of trial of criminal cases by compurgation and by ordeal, action was taken on a presumption of guilt and the burden was on the accused to purge himself. When the change was made which placed the burden of proof on the state, no doubt the prior placing of the burden on the accused lingered in many minds. Instruction on presumption of innocence would remind jurors of the change.

Few people understand the effect of the plea of *nolo contendere* in criminal cases. Assuming that the accused is a first offender and that he is guilty, he is faced with the initial question of how to plead. If he pleads not guilty and elects to stand trial, he does so in the hope that some fortuitous circumstance will arise whereby he can secure a verdict of not guilty. Further, he is showing defiance of law and a complete absence of repentance. He is causing the county great expense and is wasting the time of the court. After he has been proven to be guilty he appears with his lawyer for sentencing. Then his lawyer makes a plea for leniency. Judges get worn out with the repetitious nature of these pleas. They generally fall on deaf ears because they are hollow.

On the other hand, if the accused pleads *nolo contendere,* or perhaps guilty, he shows acceptance of law, a willingness to abide by a proper penalty, and a repentant attitude. Further, he has not caused the expense to the county, and he has freed the time of the court to other necessary tasks. When he appears for sentencing the judge is more likely to be receptive to his lawyer's plea for leniency. The law is as interested in restoration of a sense of civic responsibility as it is in inflicting punishment. The sentence imposed will undoubtedly be substantially lighter.

A recent survey in one of our larger cities disclosed that approximately thirty per cent of indictments actually went to trial. Yet the congestion in our courts is so great that it is difficult for the courts to give speedy trials, as they are constitutionally required to do. There is sound reason to believe that if the accused, his lawyer, and his family will earnestly consider a plea of *nolo contendere,* it will be used more often and the congestion in our criminal courts and the crowding of our jails will be reduced.

6

Actors in the Drama

THIS is a book about juries. But there are other participants in every trial: lawyers, judges, and witnesses. Before describing the conduct of a trial, we will pause here and discuss very briefly these special members of the trial's *dramatis personae*.

A plaintiff or a defendant needs no particular qualification; he or she is an ordinary person who is in the courtroom in search of justice. The guides along the pathway to justice are specially qualified men, or women. Together, these guides— these lawyers, these judges—form the framework within which the trial is conducted and the witnesses are heard.

First, let us look at what is a lawyer.

A lawyer receives his authority to practice law by virtue of having been admitted to practice in a court which is authorized to admit candidates. This authority extends over the area of which the court has jurisdiction. He is an officer of the court and subject to its legal orders, and as such, he is not subject to arrest while attending court in litigation or while going to or coming from court. In his relation with clients, he must exercise the utmost integrity, fidelity, honesty, and good faith. He must possess that degree of legal skill and knowledge ordinarily present in his fellow practitioners. He cannot serve two masters who have conflicting interests. He must not stir up litigation or chase ambulances. He must act within the authority granted by his client and must not violate his client's instructions. He must not reveal information given by a client in confidence.

When engaged in litigation a lawyer has authority to act in prosecution and management of the case, and he must diligently prosecute and defend regardless of remuneration and regardless of his own opinion of guilt or liability. He is neither judge nor juror. His sole duty is to promote and advance the interests of his client, and to use skill and diligence in securing a verdict for his client. He can withdraw from a case only with the judge's permission, but he can be discharged at any time. He is liable for damages caused his client by his negligence. He is entitled to a retainer fee and to the value of his services, unless he is discharged with good cause. He has a lien on the papers in a suit until paid, or ordered by the judge to return them. He must represent an indigent person, if appointed by the judge. He is subject to disbarment, either permanently or for a set time, for misconduct.

The client is entitled to assistance from his lawyer at every step of the trial. The client cannot complain of the competence of a lawyer whom he selected, but, if represented by an assigned lawyer, he can base an appeal on the incompetence of the lawyer.

The trial is conducted by the lawyers for the respective litigants. The lawyers decide which witnesses to call and the order in which they will testify. Each lawyer takes a calculated risk when he calls a witness to testify, for the witness may not testify in accord with the lawyer's expectation. Yet, the lawyer is bound by the testimony of his witness. He cannot impeach his own witness. He can call another witness who will contradict the prior witness. But the ill effects of the testimony of the unsatisfactory witness may be difficult to overcome, and certainly they cannot be obliterated. Thus, the decision on which witnesses to call is not always easy to make.

Lawyers conduct the examinations of witnesses, present argument to the judge on matters of law, and finally present argument to the jury on matters of fact.

Lawyers are strictly advocates for their clients. It is no part of their duty to weigh the evidence they present, nor are they supposed to pass upon the credibility of the witnesses whom they call. These are functions of the jury.

The vast expansion of the field of law brought about by the regulatory and welfare agencies of cities, states, and nation has caused a demand for lawyers. The agencies must have lawyers. Those who do business with the agencies must have lawyers to guide them in complying with the regulations established by the agencies. The increase in the number and the size of business and commercial enterprises has brought an added demand for lawyers, trained in the relatively new fields of law, such as internal revenue and labor relations. Our law schools have been forced to expand the area of instruction to cover the fields of law brought into being by this expansion. This expansion, however, has not significantly increased the number of jury trials. The result is that law schools have a lessening demand for instruction in jury trial work.

Law schools are operated not for the benefit of the public, but to instruct in the fields of practice which students intend to follow. As only a minority of students intend to undertake jury trial work, it is but natural for law schools to relegate instruction in trial work to a minor position in the curriculum. The schools do cover the fields of law embraced in jury trials—such as contracts, torts, and evidence—but they cannot allot the necessary time to train students in the practical aspects of jury trials. The result is that a beginner in trial work must learn how to try cases in one of two ways. The more brash undertake trial work immediately, in the hope of learning by experience. This method often tests the patience of judges and jurors. More prudent young men understudy to active trial lawyers for a year or two.

Judges in federal courts are appointed for life in order to make them independent. In most states, judges in state courts are elected; in the rest of the states, they are appointed, nominally by the governor. Both methods involve party politics to some extent. So, with few exceptions, lawyers seek judgeships. That fact has the advantages that judgeships are acquired by men who are fully aware of the responsibilities of the office, feel that they can adequately perform, and have a strong desire to perform. Either system works out to the satisfaction of the public, except in instances where a city political machine is strong enough to elect any candidate. Almost without exception some screening process precedes selection of candidates. Screening can avert the presence of obvious misfits. However, no screening process can be relied upon to produce competent judges, because proof of competence comes only after the judge takes office.

The care with which candidates are selected does help toward getting able judges. However, there is a natural human quality which has much more bearing and on which great reliance can be based. That is the human quality of pride, or, if you will, self-esteem. Any judge upon assuming the duties of his office is the object of close scrutiny by his fellow judges and by the lawyers who appear before him. This scrutiny results in his being graded by them in some category from excellent to poor. The collective opinion of these men establishes the reputation of the new judge. Pride compels him to make an effort to be placed, by repute, in the highest grade which he can attain. Any elected judge knows that if he desires re-election he must run on his record. Failure of re-election is a calamity which is hard for him to face; his pride is shaken. The possibility of this calamity is a compelling force underlying judicial conduct.

Many people wonder if and how the acts of judges in the conduct of jury trials are influenced by their political associations and by their friendship with a litigant or lawyer. Many think that these possible influences may affect the judge's conduct of a trial. Let us clear up any uncertainty in this regard. In the first place, if a judge thinks that the presence of any of these influences may be construed as having an influence on his actions, he will have the trial transferred to another judge. He feels no obligation to favor anybody. Indeed, should he show favor he would be subject to harsh criticism, such as is due to one who violates solid tradition. If there be political or social obligations, they can be discharged in a perfectly proper manner. All judges, from time to time, have the opportunity to make appointments of such officials as receivers, trustees, and guardians. Almost any experienced lawyer can fill these appointments, which can be used to balance the judge's political and social accounts, and without detriment to anyone.

The scenario writers for television shows of jury trials aim to produce entertainment. In doing so they exclude the un-entertaining features of trials. Perhaps the greatest false impression given to the public is that of the functions of judges. They portray the judge's duties as such a sinecure that all men should envy the holding of such an easy job at a high salary. The reader will soon learn of the serious and difficult duties connected with conducting jury trials. Not the least of these is the application of sound discretion in the disposition of many details which are entrusted to the judge's discretion.

In addition to presiding at jury trials, a judge must rule on many matters which come up before and after trials. He must conduct non-jury trials. He must conduct the trials of matters which are classed as "equity," that is, non-jury trials involving such matters as injunctions. He presides at trials involving wills. He must try cases involving matrimonial relations and trials involving penal acts of minors. He must supervise the administration of estates of incompetent and deceased persons. He has many other duties. Judgeships are not sinecures. In order to perform these duties a judge must have the ability quickly to grasp issues of fact and issues of law and dispose of them promptly.

Also assembled for the trial are persons who have been called to testify—witnesses—and persons merely interested in the trial—spectators. Any person is free to attend a trial as a spectator, if and as he pleases. Any person voluntarily in the courtroom while the judge is sitting is under the jurisdiction of the judge. Thus, on request of either party that a spectator be detained as a witness, the judge may order him to remain until called to testify, or the judge may issue a subpoena forth-with and have it served on the person in the courtroom or nearby.

Any person can offer to or agree to attend trial as a voluntary witness. But no person can be compelled to attend a trial unless he has been served with a subpoena, which summons the person to attend at a definite time and place and to remain until relieved. The person summoned is entitled to travel expense and a witness fee. The amount to be paid and the time of payment are set by statute. The subpoena must be served by a person authorized by statute to do so (usually the sheriff or marshal), who delivers a true copy and makes an entry on the original that it was served.

If the subpoena is served on the person, the person must respond. If he does not do so, the party wanting him can ask the judge that he be brought in by an arresting officer, forceably if necessary. The person can be held in contempt of court with a possible penalty of fine or imprisonment, and in most states he can be sued for any damage he may have caused the party who had the subpoena issued.

The subpoena may call for him to bring to court certain papers, books, or other items of evidence. This is called a *subpoena ducas tecum*. In order to avert abuse, it is generally required that a judge authorize the issuance of this subpoena. In this way the scope and volume of material are controlled. If the subpoena calls for bulky material, arrangements will be made for transportation.

Anyone is subject to subpoena, with the exception that in a couple of states women are excused, unless it be shown that their presence is essential. The President of the United States need not respond to a subpoena. The governors of states need not respond to state court subpoenas. With such limited exceptions, all persons must respond to a subpoena who are physically and mentally able to do so. A person may, however, evade service without penalty.

Witnesses may not be present at the trial and yet still be able to testify. This is accomplished through depositions. The taking of depositions is a development by statute during this century. The details vary from state to state to such an extent that here it is possible to give only a broad picture of this practice and to describe the practice in general terms. Use of depositions in criminal cases is so limited in scope and so little used that it will be passed over.

A deposition is testimony of parties and witnesses under oath in civil actions taken anywhere in the world by written questions or by oral testimony before an officer with certain prescribed qualifications, including the authority to administer the oath. It is then reduced to writing. The general purposes are discovery of facts, the preservation of testimony, to qualify evidence from outside the jurisdiction to be used in a trial, and to avoid surprise testimony at a trial.

Depositions by written interrogatories are taken in this way: One party notifies the other party that it is taking the deposition of a certain person and submits the questions, reasonable in number, which he proposes to ask. The other side then adds whatever questions it desires to have answered. The questions are then sent to the designated officer, most often a notary public, who propounds the questions to the witness, and writes the answers. Depositions by written interrogatories are a great help to the parties if the questions can be drafted so as to pinpoint an answer to yes or no. Otherwise, answers can be so given that they supply little information of value. This fact is a drawback to the use of written interrogatories.

Depositions taken by oral examination are taken in this way: The witness, the lawyers, and a court reporter meet at a designated time and place. Usually, the meeting is held in the office of one of the lawyers and in a rather informal manner. The questions are asked, answered, and recorded. The rules of evidence do not apply. Any questions are permitted which have any relevancy. The questions can cover the disclosure of facts, exhibits, and possible witnesses. Hearsay evidence and opinions evidence are proper. In fact, the scope of examination is so broad that the process is also designated "discovery." If a dispute arises as to the propriety of any question or questions asked, the witness can refuse to answer until a judge decides whether he should.

The depositions can be used in a trial to contradict a witness and to present the testimony of witnesses who, for one reason or another, are unable to attend a trial, including those who are beyond the jurisdictional limits of the court. Used to the maximum extent permitted, depositions on oral examinations can expose in writing practically all the evidence which can be presented in a trial. The practical limitation on these depositions is the cost, as there can be great expense to the party initiating the deposition.

At the common law the right to take depositions was unknown. This right is strictly statutory. The provisions of the statutes must be substantially followed in all particulars. In civil cases the statutes allow liberal use of depositions by written interrogatories and by oral examination. In criminal cases the statutes must not be in conflict with the right of the accused to be confronted by witnesses for the prosecution. For this reason some states prohibit the prosecution from taking depositions. Other states allow depositions to be taken under restrictions which safeguard the rights of the accused. One restriction may be a requirement that a judge be satisfied of the necessity for the depositions. Then an order must be signed by the judge which places limits on the questions propounded, or the subjects to be covered by questions.

Where should witnesses wait pending call to testify? In the early days, when trials were a matter of more public concern and when courthouse facilities were limited, witnesses awaiting their turn were allowed to sit in the courtroom. Some judges continue this practice either in special instances or as a general policy. One judicial view is that witnesses have a keen interest in the facts and should not be excluded from the courtroom. One apparent benefit of this practice is that a witness will be more careful if his testimony is heard by other witnesses who may alter or contradict it. Also the memory of a witness may be sharpened by his hearing some important details he might not otherwise recollect. On the other hand, other judges exclude witnesses from the courtroom until they have testified. This practice prevents a witness from being influenced by prior testimony and from being able to alter his testimony to conform to that of prior witnesses. Neither practice is ideal for general use, so the choice is left to the discretion of the judge.

A lawyer has much freedom in deciding which witnesses he will call upon to testify. But there are some rules to which he must conform. In a civil case, if a party is shown to possess or have control of pertinent evidence and fails to produce the evidence, a jury may infer that the evidence, had it been given, would have been prejudicial to the party. The same principle applies to failure to call a witness who is under the control of the party and is probably in possession of material evidence or able to give material testimony. In criminal cases, the general rule is that the prosecution need not call all available witnesses. However, the judge may order the prosecution to call a witness, or he may order the names of prospective witnesses to be given to the defendant's lawyer. Usually, the prosecution is required to have all available eyewitnesses in court, subject to call by the defendant. The defendant is under no obligation to call witnesses.

Expert witnesses can be called like ordinary witnesses and asked about facts in the case, but they need not express their expert opinion. If an expert's opinion is wanted, arrangements as to time of appearance and remuneration should be made before the experts come to court. An expert can be asked in the trial the amount of his fee.

A lawyer may communicate with witnesses at any time before the witness is called to testify. Also, witnesses may communicate during any recess in the trial. However, if the examination of a witness has begun, the judge can, and usually does, instruct the witness not to communicate with any person who is in any way connected with the trial. A witness called by one side can be used by the other side.

The immunity of witnesses against self-incrimination is specifically granted in federal courts by the Fifth Amendment to the Constitution of the United States, which provides that no person "shall be compelled in any criminal case to be a witness against himself." Although the amendment is stated to apply in criminal cases, the courts have construed it to apply to all court proceedings and to confessions. It applies in order to protect against any self-disclosures which may lead to prosecution and punishment. It does not apply if the disclosure leads merely to embarrassment or disgrace or subjects a person to civil liability. It applies equally in direct examination, cross-examination, and in the production of papers and other items of evidence. The amendment uses the word *compelled,* which means that the immunity may be waived. An accused who takes the witness stand, which he is not obligated to do, automatically waives the immunity and is subject to cross-examination. If an ordinary witness is asked a question whose answer would incriminate him, he has the right to refuse to answer the question by claiming the privilege of the Fifth Amendment.

In 1965, the United States Supreme Court held that the Fifth Amendment applied in both federal and state courts.

In federal courts, and in most state courts, this immunity is construed to extend to a prohibition against the prosecutor's commenting to the jury on the defendant's failure to testify. In these courts, the judge is required or permitted to instruct the jury that the defendant's failure to testify shall not be held against him.

Immunity is particularly important when applied to confessions. A person under arrest is perfectly free to make a confession. However, not all confessions are admissible in evidence. In order to be admissible a confession must be a voluntary act. It must be clearly free from duress or inducement of any sort. Otherwise, it is regarded as unreliable and therefore inadmissible. Some states provide additional safeguards by statutes which require that an accused receive warning that any confession may be used against him. Then, in the absence of such warning, the confession is not admissible.

Immunity also exists as to items of real evidence. The Fourth Amendment to the Constitution of the United States provides that persons are "secure in their persons, houses, papers, and effects against searches and seizures, and no Warrant shall issue, but upon reasonable cause." This means that the right to privacy cannot be invaded in search of items of real evidence and the fruit thereof used in court against the defendant. A like provision is in state constitutions. So a person has immunity in his person and home against search for incriminating evidence, unless it is first shown to a judge that probable cause exists, and a search warrant is lawfully issued. In times past, invasions of the right to privacy involved actual invasions. Nowadays, judges may be obligated to rule on the legality of various means of electronic eavesdropping and the use of evidence so acquired.

What right does a witness have to withhold testimony about confidential matters? Under the common law, a husband or wife was incompetent to testify for or against the other spouse. This rule has been greatly relaxed by statute. Some states retain the rule in criminal trials but only as to testimony against the spouse; other states abrogate the rule entirely. No general rule is applicable. In almost all states the rule is that communications between husband and wife which are made in the confidence of the marital relation are not admissible. Neither spouse is allowed to disclose them unless the other spouse waives the privilege.

Lawyers are not permitted to testify regarding disclosures made to them in the confidence of the relationship of lawyer and client.

In order to be privileged, the communication must meet four tests. It must originate in the confidence that it will remain secret; the element of confidentiality must be essential to the relationship between the parties; the relationship must be one which the community believes should be fostered; and the injury to the relationship by the disclosure must be greater than the benefit gained for the correct disposition of the litigation. It is generally assumed that confidential relations exist between but two parties and that the presence of a third party destroys the confidential relation. This is not strictly true. There can be circumstances which so justify the presence of a third party that the confidential relationship is not destroyed.

A clergyman who testifies in court has extraordinary rights as a witness today. But this has not always been true. At the common law, confessions of sin made to a spiritual adviser were admissible. The application of this rule did not seem fair and proper to many people, especially in instances of confessions made under sect obligation. As a result, in many states statutes provide that confessions made to a priest or minister acting in that capacity will not be accepted as evidence if made by a penitent person in the expectation of spiritual aid in conformity with belief.

7

The Trial Opens

A TRIAL is opened with a statement by one of the lawyers in which he briefly outlines the facts which he expects to prove. Then he will say that, if the jury finds the facts to be as stated by him, he will request a verdict for his party.

The party who has the affirmative, that is, the party who has the burden of proof, is entitled to make the opening statement. In civil cases the lawyer for plaintiff almost always makes the opening statement. If a question arises as to which civil litigant has the affirmative, the decision will rest with the judge. He decides on the basis of which party would be entitled to a verdict if no evidence were introduced. This is done by examining the pleadings. Usually it is found that the verdict would go to the defendant and so the affirmative is with the plaintiff. His lawyer is not permitted to forego an opening statement.

If each party makes claim against the other, the opening statement will be by the party who initiated the action. If, therefore, a situation exists wherein it is known that there are claims by both parties, it is advantageous to be the one first to file suit.

An opening statement contains an outline of the case without recitation of all details. However, it must be sufficient in breadth to include the necessary facts which constitute a case. The statement should inform the jury who the parties are and what their relationship is to the case; the series of acts and actions which will be revealed by the evidence; a description of the exhibits which will be introduced; the logical conclusion based on the evidence; and what jury action should result from the conclusion. The opening statement will be in the nature of a pledge to show certain facts and conditions. This pledge can be carried out in good faith only by making promises that can be fulfilled.

Since the word "case" will be used often in this book, it is appropriate to define the word at this point. Each criminal and civil case must show certain essential facts in order to constitute a lawful charge or claim, and each essential fact is comparable to a link in a chain. If the opening statement contains these facts, it is effective and will impress the jury; if it does not contain one or more of the essential facts, a link in the chain is missing, and so a lawful claim or charge has not been stated.

Let us take a concrete example and consider a case of fraud that is brought by a plaintiff. This case is made up of eight elements or essential facts. These are: a *representation* (or claim) (1) . . . which is *false* (2) . . . relating to a *material matter* (3) . . . upon which the plaintiff has a *right to rely* (4) . . . and which the defendant *knows to be false* (or is recklessly heedless of the truth or falsity) (5) . . . at a time when plaintiff is *ignorant of the falsity* (6) . . . but upon which he nevertheless *relies* (7) . . . and, as a result of his reliance, he *suffers an injury* (8). If the plaintiff fails to assert any one element or essential fact he has not stated a case.

In a criminal case, the prosecutor makes the opening statement. In some states he is permitted to forego making an opening statement, but he will seldom do so. He too must present all the elements necessary to state a case. This includes the element of intent.

Occasionally, the lawyer for the defendant, in either type of case, thinks that the statement does not include the facts necessary to constitute a lawful case. In that event, he will "move that a directed verdict be entered for defendant." This motion, as it is called, requires the judge to determine whether the opening statement does state a "case."

If the judge "sustains" the motion, that is, agrees with defendant's lawyer, he may, in a civil case, give the plaintiff's lawyer the privilege of amending his statement in an effort to have it state a case, or, in both types of cases, he will go through the formality of directing a verdict for the defendant. If the judge "overrules" the motion, which indicates that he does not agree with defendant's lawyer, the trial will proceed.

The fact that the trial proceeds does not always overcome tactical damage to plaintiff. The jury may have received an impression that the lawyer does not know and has not prepared his case, has not thought the case of sufficient importance to prepare an adequate statement, or is careless in not following the outline of his case as stated in the complaint.

All too often, in making the opening statement, the lawyer for the affirmative side concentrates attention on stating a case which will meet the legal tests just outlined, and glides over the two basic objectives of the opening statement. These basic objectives are, first, to inform the jury plainly, accurately, and understandably in what way the defendant was wrong. (It means little to state that the defendant was negligent in failing to stop at a crossing. It means much if, in addition, it is stated that he violated a traffic ordinance to make a full stop at a stop sign.) The second basic objective is to inform the jury plainly, precisely, and fully of the items of damage or the precise criminal charge for which a verdict is sought. When these two objectives are known and understood by the jury, the jury's task is made easier, since the evidence of each witness can then be related to these objectives.

After the affirmative lawyer has finished, the opposing lawyer may make a similar statement outlining the defense. He usually makes his statement at this time, but he may defer it until the affirmative lawyer has completed presenting evidence to support his case.

A jury should have more than a narrative of a series of events, such as one could read in a newspaper. As jurors are involved with issues of fact, they must understand at some time, and the sooner the better, exactly what are the issues of fact which they are called upon to decide.

One would expect that a requirement so simple would be met, yet often it is not met. Take, for instance, this actual case. A man, after sitting on a jury for a day and a half, was asked what the trial was about. He answered: "It's a dispute between a landlord and a tenant. But I don't know yet what it is about."

Because of the difference in the burden of proof in the two types of cases, a jury can expect that in civil trials both sides will make statements at the beginning of the trial. A jury can expect that in criminal trials no opening statement will be made by the defense.

Up to this point, opening statements have been described as steps in procedure. It might appear that the statements are comparable to a formula like $2 + 2 = 4$, and, having established the 2's, the sum of 4 will result. The peculiarity of jurors is that each 2 set forth by the lawyer as static is received by each juror as fluid, so that a 2 may be 2, -2, or $+2$. The result of adding fluid 2's is not necessarily 4.

Statements of the lawyers are not transmitted to minds reposing in a vacuum. They are received into minds which contain a heterogeneous mass of ideas created by previous perceptions mixed up with all sorts of emotions present in various strengths. Each statement of fact triggers a response from the mass of mind material which William James once described as a "blooming, buzzing confusion." The lawyers can be expected to aim to get the facts through to each of the jurors' minds so that they are *comprehended* in the manner intended. This sometimes calls for repetition and sometimes for restatement in different words.

The most important concept to each mind is that expressed by the one-letter word *I*. All acts recited to a juror are related in his mind to his *I* concept. The persistent question in a juror's mind is: "What would *I* have done?" and what the parties did is related to what a juror thinks that *he* would have done in like circumstances. This question, as framed, is not proper; the proper question is: "What would the ordinary reasonable man have done?" But, since a juror views himself as an ordinary reasonable man, the question becomes appropriate on that basis.

The problem then of making an opening statement is not

only to state a case, or to recite facts which satisfy the speaker's concept of logic. Rather his problem is to state the facts that will secure a favorable response, or to state facts in such words and in such a setting that they will secure a favorable response. By favorable response is meant that each juror will respond properly to the persistent question, *"I* would have acted in the same way."

The opening statements give the lawyers their first opportunity to present to the jury the information upon which each juror will decide his ultimate answer to the persistent question, "What would *I,* as an ordinary reasonable man, have done?" The whole trial will be directed toward supplying the ultimate answer to this question.

Opening statements can be planned to affect the severity of the penalty, or the amount of liability, if the verdict should be adverse to the defendant. The public tolerates a certain amount of crime, but becomes demanding when the number of crimes passes a certain point. The toleration limit is lower for some crimes than for others. A few examples of contrasting situations are in order. A first offender as against a repeater. A thief for bread to feed a family as against a thief by occupation. An underpaid embezzler from an opulent employer as against embezzlement for fast living. A little local gambler as against a member of a gambling syndicate. A lone abortionist as against a member of a ring. This point was brought out in a case in which a doctor, not a member of a ring, was tried on a charge of having performed a non-fatal abortion. Some time after the trial one of the jurors said, "As soon as we heard the charge we were going to let the doctor off. But his lawyer raised such a hallabaloo and got so much newspaper publicity that we had to find the doctor guilty." Consider the effect of showing in the persons engaged in the trial their relative qualities of avarice, deception, malingering, shrewdness, craftiness, vindictiveness, and malice. These factors are proper to mention if evidence will be presented to establish them.

Words are used to express thoughts. Misunderstandings are often due to persons not having equal and uniform word sense.

There is an assumption, carelessly formed, that our hearers understand our words in the sense that we expect them to be understood. Our hearers are hesitant to expose any lack of understanding. The English language has its limitations of preciseness, and people have limitations in the use of English. The average person uses about six hundred words in daily conversation. His very limited vocabulary and limited understanding of the real meaning of many words which he uses can cause confusion. The lawyer uses words according to his word sense, while a juror hears words according to his word sense and may give them a meaning quite different than that intended. When word sense is not uniform, the lawyer has failed to accurately convey thought. Therefore, a lawyer should make certain that jurors understand his words in the sense intended. The problem of word understanding is emphasized when we consider that all persons connected with a trial should be in agreement as to the intended meaning of each word.

At the opening of this chapter, it was said that the lawyers will outline the facts they intend to prove. Obviously, both parties cannot carry out their intent. One party or the other will fail. Trials are based on hope. It would, therefore, be more accurate had the lawyers said they hoped to prove rather than expected to prove. This is necessarily true because lawyers experience disappointments in that witnesses fail to appear, fail to testify as expected, and reveal facts which are unknown to the lawyers who call them to the stand.

8

What Is Evidence?

EVIDENCE includes every means by which facts are established or disproved—whether by oral testimony, writings, photographs, or objects. Testimony is evidence, but refers to oral statements made under oath during a trial.

The plaintiff, or the state, naturally puts on evidence first. Usually the plaintiff or the prosecuting witness, if there be one, is the first person to be called to testify. The first witness is called and takes an oath or affirmation to tell the truth, the whole truth, and nothing but the truth.

This oath is given by placing a hand on a Bible. At the common law the oath was mandatory and generally the witness was required to kiss the Bible. This requirement excluded testimony from atheists because they had no belief in the Bible, young children because they had not personally acquired belief, and adults whose faith prohibited oaths. These old requirements were abandoned after the year 1800. The requirement to kiss the Bible was abandoned as unsanitary. As a substitute, a hand is placed on the Bible. Non-Christians take the oath on something sacred to them. An Arab will swear by the Koran, and Chinese have taken the oath by breaking a saucer. Others are now permitted to make a declaration. Children are qualified if they know right from wrong and know that they should tell the truth. Unfortunately, too many witnesses take the oath in a perfunctory manner. There was, for instance, the woman who was to be her friend's principal witness in a divorce suit. They went to a lawyer's office to discuss the case prior to trial. The woman blandly asked the lawyer: "What do you want me to testify?"

Measures can be taken to add force to the oath, the simplest of which might be to instruct children in the meaning of the precaution stated by George Washington in his Farewell Address: "Let it simply be asked where is the security for property, for reputation, for life, if the sense of religious obligation desert the oaths, which are the instruments of investigation in Courts of Justice?"

The testimony brought about by questions of the lawyer who calls (first questions) the witness is called direct testimony. It is so called because the lawyer is limited to asking direct questions. The taking of this direct testimony is spoken of as direct examination.

This testimony, and all testimony, must meet certain qualifications to insure a fair trial. Broadly speaking, all facts which have a tendency to establish the issues of fact may be used. The rules of evidence are for the most part negative and relate to what testimony is not admissible. These negations, or we might say limitations, require that the lawyers limit themselves to questions which meet all three requirements of being relevant, material, and competent.

By *relevant* is meant that the evidence has some logical relations to the issues in dispute.

By *material* is meant that the evidence is relevant and refers to substantial evidence, neither too remote in time, uncertain, nor conjectured.

By *competent* is meant that the evidence is fit, appropriate, and acceptable under the rules of evidence.

A trial is carried on without the jury being informed of and, therefore, not aware of these distinctions. And if no objection is voiced to questions a jury may get quite a bit of evidence which could have been but was not excluded. A juror should use his good sense in ignoring what he regards as being irrelevant, immaterial, and incompetent, and should reject such testimony in his deliberations.

A few illustrations will point up these three qualifications.

In an action for slander, evidence that the defendant lost another suit for slander two years ago is not relevant. In proving

73

earning power lost by reason of an accident, a man's earning power five years before the accident is not relevant because circumstances have changed.

In a case wherein negligence was charged to a station agent for failing to warn of an approaching train a woman who had defective vision but who did not wear glasses, questions regarding the woman's eyesight were immaterial because the agent did not know of her frailty at the time of the incident. A question to an undertaker as to whether a man accused of murdering a girl friend paid for the casket in which the victim was buried was immaterial, since several factors, other than a sense of guilt, might have prompted the purchase. In a case involving a policeman on trial on a charge of misconduct, questions to disclose that other policemen did the same act are incompetent.

Questions that are not proper include: all questions calling for answers based on hearsay, some calling for opinions, and all questions that are leading, in that the questions themselves suggest the answers. (Hearsay is excluded because the originator of the hearsay is not present and subject to cross-examination. Opinions, except by experts on a subject, are improper because, being conclusions, they invade the jury's province.)

The trial judge has no duty to voice objections to questions which are improper. He will interpose, however, if the questions are obnoxious or abusive. He also may interpose if he thinks questions are repetitious or are causing unnecessary delay.

The lawyer for the other side has the right to object to questions which he thinks are improper. If improper questions are asked and answered without objection, the questions and answers are evidence in the case.

In making objection to a question, the lawyer who is not questioning the witness will exclaim, "I object!" The witness is supposed not to answer. The judge may then require the objecting lawyer to state the grounds of his objection. The judge then rules whether the question is to be answered by the witness.

If the judge rules that the objection is well grounded, he will *sustain* it. This rules the question out. Otherwise, he will *overrule* the objection. This ruling allows the question to be answered. The lawyer who made the objection may then say, "Exception" (meaning: "I do not accept the ruling."). This exception can later be the basis of an appeal to the proper appellate court. The appellate court may find that the judge was wrong in his ruling and, if the judge's error is ruled to have prejudiced the jury, may send the case back to the trial court for a new trial.

Consider now the situation of the lawyer when an objection to his question is sustained, so that an answer is not recorded. An appellate court will say that it cannot pass on the question of admissibility in the absence of knowledge of the evidence ruled out by the trial judge. If the excluded evidence is so important that the lawyer desires to protect his right to appeal, he will state that he wishes to offer proof. Then, generally in the absence of the jury, he will state for the record the facts which he would have established if the objection had not been sustained. He will also show the materiality, competency, and relevancy of the evidence offered. The important thing is the certainty that the offer of proof is preserved in the record of the trial.

Laymen are often perplexed when the judge prohibits certain questions from being asked. The trial judge, in making his ruling, does not do so merely as his personal desire dictates. The judge is bound by well-established rules of evidence, rules that are themselves part and parcel of the common law or the statute law. In other words, testimony and evidence are themselves controlled by the law of evidence. The judge is bound by these rules. He determines, by the law of evidence, whether a question is legally proper and the answer properly presentable as testimony in the case.

During the course of a trial, many questions which are technically improper are not objected to for one reason or another. For example, a woman will be called as a witness and the first question may be "Are you the wife of the defendant?" This is a leading question and is technically objectionable. The relationship would be properly established by asking "Are you related in any way to the defendant?" Yet it would seem inane

75

to object to the question as first framed because the difference in effect is trifling. As the trial goes on, many similar questions will be asked in the interest of shortening a trial. If they were all objected to, jurors would get disgusted and perhaps insulted that they were credited with so little intelligence as not to recognize the question and answer as of so little importance that an objection causes only unnecessary interruption. The usual practice is to pass over such objections and make objections only to questions of some significance.

A positive reason for not voicing an objection is that the question and answer may open up an opportunity for the other side to go in detail into matters which are improper but much to his advantage. As an example:

In a murder trial, the prosecutor asked an irrelevant question: Did the defendant and the deceased have a difficulty about two weeks before the homicide, and had not the defendant at that time struck the deceased with a hoe? The defendant's lawyer made no objection to the question. Later, in his testimony, the defendant was asked by his lawyer if the deceased did not bring on the difficulty at the time he was struck with the hoe by attacking the defendant in the defendant's home. The trial judge sustained objection to this question, and this ruling was appealed. The appellate court held that the prosecutor's question was improper but that it opened the way for the defendant's lawyer to bring out the circumstances under which the hoe was used. The conviction was set aside.

Lawyers, presumably being experienced and well grounded in the law of evidence, should be able to refrain from asking questions which are clearly improper, and from voicing objection to questions which are clearly proper. If they so act, the objections on which the judge must rule will be limited to those that present a close decision. The trial will then be orderly.

It is not safe to assume, however, that all lawyers and litigants desire an orderly trial. At times, improper questions are knowingly asked just to cause an objection and perhaps a resulting, diverting wrangle. At other times, objections will be made which are knowingly without a valid reason and which bring about a wrangle. It is difficult for jurors to determine which lawyer is the cause of the disorder. The jury is, however, witness to the conduct of each lawyer and tends to be drawn into making a decision in a mere lawyers' battle. That is not its function, however. Its function is to await and abide by the ruling of the trial judge on the admissibility of the evidence about which the lawyers have disagreed.

It is not unusual for a witness to answer a question before the lawyer for the opposite side has a chance to voice his objection. If the answer is of little importance, the episode will likely be passed over with a caution by the judge to the witness not to repeat this offense. If the answer is of substantial importance, the opposing lawyer will ask the judge to have the answer stricken. If this motion is granted, the judge will usually instruct the jury specifically to ignore the question and the answer.

Questions addressed to a witness naturally call for an answer. There are a few rules which apply to answers. We will consider the two rules which are most often applied.

First, an answer must be responsive to the question. Answers are often not responsive, due perhaps to lack of clarity or to a misunderstanding of the question. It may, too, be due to intentional evasion. At times it is due to a desire on the part of the witness to inject entirely improper testimony.

Second, a witness is entitled to give an answer which is full and complete. His answer cannot be cut off short, thereby becoming misleading and not truly responsive.

These two rules involve duty and right. The duty of a witness is to be responsive, the right is to be fully responsive. These facts confuse some witnesses who feel that a responsive and full answer seems to call for hearsay testimony and perhaps for opinions or conclusions. In everyday life, there is no requirement that statements be based on fact, or that they be made with the knowledge of the event being talked about. We acquire most of our information from newspapers, conversations, and other sources without having occasion to be greatly concerned with accuracy. We are seldom called upon to differentiate between what we *know* to be true and what we have *accepted* as true. The situation is different when we testify in court. There truth is demanded, so a witness may testify only to what he knows from personal experience, regardless of the prestige of other sources of information. The objection to hearsay testimony is not based on an assumption that it has no value. Rather, it is based on the fact that the source of hearsay information is not subject to cross-examination as to its accuracy.

Hearsay testimony can be of great value. We use the expression that where there is smoke there is fire. So in gathering evidence to support a court action, hearsay indicates that there is some basis which gives rise to the hearsay. However, the courtroom is not the place to attempt to discover evidence which supports hearsay. A procedural way to do that is provided. That way is by deposition, a process which is explained on page 60.

The opinions and conclusions of witnesses are sometimes said to be inadmissible on the basis that it is a jury function to form opinions and to reach conclusions. This statement is too broad. Admissibility depends on circumstances. An opinion is a belief stronger than an impression; a conclusion is a reasoned judgment. So, in a case being tried on a defense of insanity, a lay witness may testify to his opinion that from his observation the defendant was sane or insane. But a jury weighs the value of such an opinion and reaches a conclusion in the issue of sanity based on all the evidence. The layman's opinion is admissible because it is of possible aid to the jury in reaching a conclusion. On the other hand, a layman's opinion of defendant's guilt is not an aid to a jury, and is therefore ruled out.

Opinions are admissible which go to the question of motivation. For example, the defense on a charge of assault may be that the defendant observed that the accuser made a movement of his right hand toward a pocket and this led the accused to the opinion that the accuser was about to draw a weapon. As another example, in a fraud case the person defrauded must have formed an opinion that the defrauder was trustworthy.

It is appropriate, under the subject of the taking of evidence, to give some consideration to the manner of giving testimony.

A litigant has practically no influence over the manner in which supporting witnesses testify, but he does have control over the manner in which he himself testifies. Observation of litigants in many trials will lead anyone to the conclusion that only an exceptional litigant shows an understanding of his position in a trial and has prepared himself to testify. The position of a majority of litigants is comparable to that of a salesman whose approach to a prospective buyer is: "You don't want to buy this, do you?" The testimony of litigants is often on just such a negative basis and the result can be expected to be the same: no sale. A common occurrence is for a litigant who charges the defendant with negligence to convey an image of himself as a careless person who can be expected to cause the same kind of accident that is the basis of his complaint.

An intelligent and thoughtful salesman knows the worth of his wares and plans how to present them in a manner that will produce sales. A litigant may well take the time and effort to clarify and organize his thoughts so that he can present his testimony in a clear-cut and definite manner. He will also plan to use his voice properly and persuasively. A mumbling, fumbling voice carries no conviction and does not become a litigant. A litigant who prepares himself to testify will speak audibly and knowingly. Thus he will convey a definite impression that he knows what he is talking about and is convinced that what he says is worthy of belief.

Besides testimony, there is another class of evidence called demonstrative evidence. This includes all the material things which are evidence, such as bank checks, vouchers, books of account, letters, contracts, hospital reports, death certificates, diagrams, photographs, revolvers, bullets, clothing, and the like. These are known as exhibits. An exhibit is introduced in evidence by showing it to the opposing lawyer and then having the clerk of the court mark it for identification. Then the opposing lawyer is given an opportunity to voice any objection he may have. In the absence of objection, or if the judge rules against an objection, the exhibit is received in evidence and marked with a letter or number. It is then shown to the jurors. If it consists of written material the lawyer, in the interest of time, may be permitted to read it to the jury.

Exhibits have great impact because the words of the lawyers will not change the material evidence represented by the exhibit. Exhibits are prima facie evidence; that is, they are credible on their face alone. They are subject to attack, as a bank check may be attacked by a claim of forgery. All people are inclined to give full credit to exhibits but often that credit is not justified. Photographs can be processed to omit parts, and composite photographs can be made to deceive. Samples of blood and urine can be switched and mistakes can be made in analysis. Forgeries of writings and signatures can be made so cleverly as to require specialists to disprove them. Exhibits can be deliberately made which appear to be originals, but turn out to be false.

In one case, a husband and wife who operated a business were on trial for making false income tax returns over a period of years. To prove their innocence, they produced at the trial their ledger accounts for the period of years in which the evasion was charged. These ledgers showed that there had been no evasion so they were found not guilty. The prosecutor instigated further investigation. Ledger manufacturers often put a number in small type on the inside cover of a ledgerbook to show style number, and they take orders by this number. The ledger in question had such an identification number. This number was checked with the store where defendants said they had purchased the ledgers. The records of the store disclosed that the year the store had first ordered this number ledger was subsequent to the year the couple claimed they had bought it. On this evidence, the partners were convicted of perjury.

Exhibits do not stand on their own feet but are introduced into a case by means of testimony. This testimony is subject to the tests of credibility and accuracy, just as is any other testimony. In a drunken driving case, tests of urine were accepted in evidence through the persons in the police department who had handled the sample from the time it was taken until the trial. It was conclusive evidence of intoxication, yet the testimony was not accepted by the jury as credible. After the trial, one juror stated that the jurors had not believed a single witness in the case—except the policeman who, though he had made the arrest, testified that he did not believe the accused had been intoxicated. Those who handled the sample of urine and made the tests were discredited, and the accused was found not guilty.

Years ago, about 1910, a lawyer of city-wide fame in divorce cases made excellent use of a camera—and the cooperation of a clever young woman and an alert photographer. The lawyer first learned where a man to be sued for a divorce ate lunch, or attended meetings and amusements. The lawyer would have the woman visit these places and, as she left, she would artfully smile up at the man. Then flash—the photographer had a picture. With many such tricky photographs in the possession of the lawyer, it seemed foolhardy for the man to deny knowing the woman and knowing her well. The result of this practice was many uncontested divorces.

At the end of a trial, the jury may ask that the exhibits be sent to the jury room. The trial judge will then notify the lawyers of this request and will consider any objections which the lawyers may have. Unless it be shown that a party will be prejudiced or that other substantial grounds for objection exist, the exhibits will be delivered to the jury room.

There is another classification of evidence which receives no recognition from the text writers, the judges, and the appellate courts—except in an extreme case. That is the observations of jurors during a trial of events or things in the courtroom. The courts do hold, for example, that leaving the blood-stained clothing of a victim within the observation of a jury is improper, but not so improper as to call for a new trial. Matters of lesser importance receive no attention and usually do not get into the record of a trial. For instance, tears do not show up in the record. Yet they can affect the juror's appraisal of the credibility of testimony and they may affect the amount of the award.

A couple of incidents from trials will bring this point home. In a recent case, a prominent white man was on trial before a jury containing several Negroes. For no stated reason, a nationally prominent Negro from out of town appeared as a spectator at the trial. It was known that he was friendly to the defendant. This appeared to be an attempt to influence the Negoes on the jury.

In another case, a woman was testifying to establish her damage for the loss of half a dozen expensive dresses. She testified that she had bought them at a swank department store and that some had cost approximately one hundred dollars and others one hundred and twenty-five dollars. The lawyer for the defendant belittled this testimony of cost, trying to imply that the woman was exaggerating and thus was not to be believed on any count. After the jury reported a verdict in favor of the woman, one of the jurors approached her lawyer and said, "We didn't like that lawyer trying to cross her up over the cost of those dresses. I'm in the fur business and I know that the coat she was wearing cost at least thirty-five hundred dollars. We figured if she would buy such an expensive coat she would buy expensive dresses."

One day, out of curiosity, the writer entered a courtroom and saw that a case was on trial. Several men sat at the table for defense counsel. It appeared that three were lawyers and the other three employees of a large corporation, the defendant. The suit involved serious injuries to a young man. It was evident from the presence of so many highly paid people that the defendant corporation was taking a very serious view of this case, and a jury could infer that the corporation feared a large verdict. The thought struck the writer that with this showing of opulence and fear, the verdict for the plaintiff, if there was one, would be large. It was in fact the largest awarded to that date in that court.

There is no doubt but that some inexperienced jurors wonder, during the early stages of a trial, whether they can ask questions and take notes. A jury is not an investigating body. It has no obligation to ferret out truth or dig for facts. In a misapprehension of jury function, an occasional juror will feel prompted to be an inquisitor. Frequent questions by jurors can disrupt a trial, and upset the order of proof planned by the lawyers. While a juror focuses his attention on what he wants answered, he will likely miss evidence being presented. Further, his question, if uttered, may be so improper as to call for a mistrial. In any event, the question which a juror has in mind will probably be answered in due time. If, however, a juror impatiently must ask a question he should write the question and have it handed to the judge. The judge will then exercise his discretion by granting or denying the request.

Jurors should not surreptitiously go to the scene of an event involved in a trial. It is very helpful at times that a jury visit and view the scene of an accident or the actual location of an event, but it is for the judge to decide whether such viewing will be permitted. If it is permitted, the judge, jury, and lawyers will go to the scene and view it under direction of the judge.

It is not proper for a juror to take notes as the trial proceeds. His attention should be focused on hearing evidence and determing credibility. Note-taking distracts. If specific amounts are stated in testimony, those amounts will be sent to the jury during its deliberation if requested. Also, if jurors want testimony read to them from the record, the judge will arrange that the jury return to the courtroom, where the testimony will be read from the record.

When the lawyer who called the witness has ended his questioning, he will so indicate by saying to his opponent something like: "You may take the witness." If the opposing counsel accepts the invitation and takes the witness, he proceeds with a series of questions designated as *cross-examination*. This has been declared to be the best means devised to date to insure that a witness testify truthfully.

No part of a trial is as fascinating as the cross-examination. Jurors heretofore interested in the direct testimony, but a bit tired, now alert themselves and pay keen attention. They are ready to put to a test their ability to detect contradictions and inconsistencies. Television and the movies have taught that witnesses are tripped up in cross-examination. Scenario lawyers are generally successful in cross-examination, and this success is made obvious in the script. In fact, successful cross-examination is a substantial cause of interest in depicting trials because it allows the viewer to weigh credibility. He becomes a vicarious juror. We all understand that digression from correct procedure is allowed in fictional court scenes, but we do not know where distortion lies in the conduct of the actors in the scenes which we see portrayed.

There are two main objectives in cross-examination, the first being to discredit the person of the witness. The second is to discredit the testimony of the witness. To discredit the person means to show that his character is such that his entire testimony is unworthy of belief. He can be discredited by showing that he has been convicted of a felony, that his occupation is dishonorable, that he spends his time in evil environment, and that he has previously committed perjury.

To discredit the testimony of a witness questions are proper which seek to learn the keenness of his senses; the opportunity his senses had to receive impressions; his familiarity with and interest in the things sensed; what senses reacted at the same time; what distractions existed; his ability to record in memory; his ability to extract from memory; his willingness to correct himself; his knowledge of the people in the case; his personal interest in the outcome of the case; how he got into the case; his bias toward any party; inconsistencies in prior statements; his attitude to his oath; and whether he is relying on initial impressions or is relying on concepts he has created from these impressions. These are not all of the subjects which may be covered but they indicate the scope of questions available.

The invitation to take the witness is usually accepted. Some lawyers accept the invitation with definite objectives in mind. But in the run of cases, the invitation is accepted without design. There are reasons which tempt lawyers to plunge into cross-examination. In the first place, some lawyers think that they must accept, that they show weakness in not accepting. Others cannot resist the opportunity to talk. Still others accept the invitation against their better judgment, lest their clients think them to be lacking in fighting quality. Clients expect a

84

show of energy. That is what they *think* they pay for. Few of them are able to appreciate the wisdom of silence. Hence, the lawyer is propelled to show energy. So he goes through a mere rehash of the direct testimony and succeeds only in fortifying the opposition by clarifying important points which were left obscure.

An instance of talking too much occurred in a suit for fire damage to a house and contents. The plaintiff was a housewife who had had no business or court experience. Her lawyer told her that he could ask her only direct questions, that he could not help her to establish her loss by asking leading questions and that she had to bring out every item of damage without his aid. When she had concluded her testimony, she had given proof of only about sixty per cent of her damage. The defendant and his lawyer had made no examination of the damage and so knew nothing about the items of damage. The defendant had little evidence to present, so his lawyer made the most of his opportunity to cross-examine the plaintiff. He had her start a description of damages in the recreation room in the basement of the house and carried her from room to room of a three-story house and then took her on a tour of the outside of the house. This inane cross-examination enabled plaintiff to establish one hundred per cent of her damage. But it is doubtful that the defendant had any idea that the energy shown by his lawyer did only harm.

Another instance was in a suit by an architect to collect his fee for making the drawings to cover the remodeling of a large brick house. The only witnesses who appeared in the courtroom were the two litigants. The architect testified to all the necessary facts except that he did not testify, in spite of cues, to a contract fee nor to the value of his services, being content to show his copy of his bill. His testimony was completed at lunch time. At the recess for lunch, his lawyer told him he had not made a case because he had not testified to the oral contract which provided for payment to him of a set fee. He was told to bring this in on his cross-examination. He said, "Suppose there is no cross-examination." He was told that in that event he was out of luck but not to worry since the defendant's lawyer was the aggressive type and would not think of passing up a chance to cross-examine. Sure enough, within five minutes after the start of cross-examination, he was asked a question which permitted him to testify to the contract setting the fee. The defense of poor workmanship did not apply to the architect, so he secured an award due solely to the cross-examination.

In order for cross-examination to be effective, it must have definite purpose. If there be no purpose, let there be no cross-examination. In those cases of sufficient importance to warrant the expenditure of a few dollars, the deposition of any party or witness can be taken. The view of the witness afforded to the lawyer when the deposition was taken, together with a review of this deposition, will disclose those points to which fruitful cross-examination can be directed.

The lawyer in cross-examination is allowed to ask leading questions (questions which suggest the answer). Words may be put in the mouth of the witness, if the witness will permit. The scope of cross-examination is very broad. The examiner, however, must limit himself to questions which are relevant, and he must not ask questions which are argumentative.

A disinterested witness has the ordinary everyday weaknesses of humanity. He naturally hesitates to place himself in a position where his weaknesses may be brought to light. He is resentful that his worthiness and credibility are put in question. This hesitation is fortified in the knowledge that cross-examination may be short of good manners, courtesy, and consideration for his feelings.

Effective cross-examination must, at least initially, be based on the assumption that the witness believes his testimony to be truthful and sincere, and that he expects it to be accepted as true. Such of his testimony as is harmless requires no cross-examination. If some of his testimony is harmful, other witnesses may be available to contradict it, so that cross-examination may not be vital. However, if there was a harmful effect, the lawyer may like to promptly remove or minimize that effect. A frontal attack will meet with resistance and with jury response favoring the witness. Loss of face is the last thing a man wants to happen to him before an audience. The witness must be allowed to save face. Therefore, any attack on harmful testimony should be a side attack which moves step by step to sap the force of the harmful testimony.

A witness is performing a public service which is more or less unremunerative. He is entitled to fair treatment. Any witness, therefore, who thinks that he is being browbeaten can call on the judge for protection. The judge will make the distinction between browbeating and necessary digging for truth. He will protect a witness from the first but not from the second.

One bad habit which many lawyers have on cross-examination is to stand over the witness. There is a natural tendency, when attempting to convince a person, to stand as close as possible to the person. Some people explain this by claiming that every person has about him an aura much like the electric field around a magnet, that this aura sometimes has a dominating influence over persons who are near it, and that witnesses do not like to be within this aura because they feel dominated by the lawyer. This can bring about anger and confusion.

Many judges, as a matter of course, require lawyers to stand away from the witness and all judges will order the lawyer to stand away if the witness voices a protest.

Every witness should know that he is to give a responsive answer to every question and is to respond in a courteous manner. This obligation exists as to both sides of the case. When this simple fact is kept in mind and followed, no witness need have a qualm in undergoing cross-examination.

When the cross-examination is finished, the lawyer who first called the witness can again ask questions. This is called *redirect-examination*. It is used to clarify answers given to questions on cross-examination. New matters are not supposed to be introduced at this time. If they are, the witness may be subject to cross-examination concerning the new matters.

Both sides having finished their questioning, the witness leaves the witness stand. He may be allowed to leave the courthouse or he may be held, subject to being recalled.

The trial then continues with the testimony of other witnesses, who are examined in the same way. These witnesses usually will be called in such order that each witness adds to the facts in terms of time, place, or condition. The order in which witnesses are called is usually left to the lawyers but is under the control of the judge. He also has authority to interrupt the testimony of a witness so as to accommodate a witness who is pressed for time and is therefore allowed to testify out of the usual order.

Mention needs to be made of participation by the trial judge in the examination of witnesses. A trial judge in the exercise of his power to govern the conduct of a trial has a duty to aid witnesses who need help in their effort to testify. Accordingly, a judge may be expected to interpose questions to a witness if the witness, in apparent good faith, is unable to comprehend a question, if he obviously has not understood the question, if he has difficulty in expressing his answer in understandable form, or when apparently contradictory answers indicate that the witness is in mental confusion. When, however, the judge participates further in the examination—as he has a perfect right to do to help establish the truth—the lawyers are apt to be offended. The examining lawyer may be particularly upset because he feels that his opponent is receiving gratuitous and unwarranted aid. Yet neither lawyer will dare interpose an objection lest he be the object of judicial wrath to the prejudice of his client in the eyes of the jury.

The prestige of the judge is such that there is a tendency on the part of jurors to give undue weight to any point on which the judge may ask questions, and to the answers elicited. When, therefore, a judge asks questions, within his discretion but outside the scope of his duty, one side or the other may claim that the judge prejudiced his case.

A more serious objection to questions by the judge is that such questioning may well interfere with the sequence of evidence which the lawyers had planned in the conduct of the trial. This is interference, in some degree, with the right of a litigant to choose his advocate. He chose his lawyer; he did not choose the judge. In the absence of unusual circumstances, the selected advocate should be permitted to present the testimony.

In almost all states, the defendant's lawyer, at the conclusion of the plaintiff's evidence, may put the plaintiff's case to an initial test by making a motion for a directed verdict in favor of the defendant. In a few states this motion cannot be made until the close of all evidence. This motion will be considered later but limited comment is necessary here.

This motion is, in effect, that the prosecutor or the plaintiff has not made a case, in that the evidence raises no issue of fact that requires jury action. If his contention is sustained, the judge will direct a verdict for the defendant because there is no evidence on which the jury can proceed. The credibility of the evidence is not tested at this time, since the judge is not concerned with the jury function of deciding facts. He is concerned with deciding a question of law: Does the evidence require jury action?

If the motion is granted, the judge will direct the jury to find for the defendant. This will be done through a form of procedure adopted for this purpose.

If the motion is overruled, and it generally is, it means that a case has been established. The case established is called a "prima facie case." Even a very feeble case may meet the test. If the defendant's lawyer wishes to preserve his right to appeal this ruling, many states require that he voice an objection. If so, he will say, "I take exception." This motion, in most states, must be repeated at the end of the trial in order to preserve the right to appeal.

The defendant is under no obligation to put on a case. He can rest on the motion and take an appeal on a claim that the judge erred in denying his motion. He participates no further in the trial, which continues without him. He will not take this action unless he is sure that he can secure a reversal in an appellate court, because he takes a chance on an adverse verdict and an affirmation of the judge's ruling. The alternative usually adopted is to proceed with the defense and, as a matter of form, repeat the motion at the end of all testimony.

It sometimes happens that on cross-examination the defendant's lawyer will introduce some evidence which is solely and exclusively defense evidence. By this act he is considered to have opened his defense. He thereby thwarts himself from making this motion at this time.

9

The Defendant's Case

THE statement that a defendant is under no obligation to put on a case requires some explanation. Initially, the defendant pleaded not guilty to the charges against him or he denied the plaintiff's claim in his answer to the complaint. That was obligatory. At that time the action of defendant's lawyer was based on an assumption that, if the case should go to trial, defense testimony would be presented. This initial defense strategy would be based on the facts as then known to the lawyer, together with such hopes and expectations as the facts seemed to justify.

In a civil case, perhaps the defendant initially feels liable to the plaintiff for damage done to his person or to his property. His lawyer could admit liability and go to trial on damages only. Why do that at this time when it is possible that additional facts may come to light and free the defendant from liability? So he will plead denial and await the development of facts. On the other hand, the defendant may feel certain that he is not liable.

In a criminal case the defendant's lawyer may feel initially that a verdict of entire non-guilt is hopeless, but that he can free the defendant on certain counts and may, through some fortuitous circumstance, get his client free. On the other hand, he may feel that available evidence will preclude a guilty verdict.

The situation is entirely different at this point in the trial from what it was at the start. The affirmative side has produced its proof and has established a prima facie case. The case will go to the jury for a verdict unless some unexpected event hap-

91

pens. Now the lawyer is obligated to weigh the factual situation presented by the affirmative and to determine whether to put on evidence in defense. In making this determination he asks himself two questions. The first is: What verdict is probable, based on the evidence presented? The second is: Will the evidence available to the defendant probably bring about a verdict more favorable to defendant? It should be obvious that, if the answer to the second question is in the negative, the lawyer should not put on a defense. Yet, time and again, the defendant's lawyer puts on a defense that brings in evidence which actually strengthens the other side's case.

Here is an example to illustrate the last point. A suit was filed which charged that an oil burner repairman had been negligent in removing surplus oil from the fire chamber of a furnace and, as one result, the house was damaged by oily smudge. At the conclusion of the plaintiff's case a motion was made for a directed verdict for the defendant. The judge, after hearing argument, said that he was inclined to grant the motion but would hold his decision until he thought the matter over during the lunch period. After lunch the judge resumed consultation with the lawyers and said that he would let the case go to the jury, but to his recollection it was the weakest case he had ever let go to a jury. That was a clear tip-off to the defendant's lawyer to let the case ride unless the defense's evidence could not possibly strengthen the plaintiff's case. It was a situation calling for consultation with the defendant to decide whether to put on evidence, put on no evidence, or try to negotiate a low settlement. But, without consultation, the lawyer called the repairman, who was his only witness. This man testified that he had been a furnace repairman for sixteen years; that he had no such previous case of damage; and that what he did in this instance was the same as he had done for sixteen years. This seemed to be an adequate defense. On cross-examination, however, he ruined the defense. He testified that his entire experience had been with heating units that had vertical pipes in the firebox; that this particular furnace had horizontal pipes; that he knew there was a dust filter; that he knew the

92

heat pipes might become hot enough to make the dirt and dust on the filter screen smolder; and that he had neither removed the filter nor even looked at it. On this testimony, there was no doubt that the case would go to the jury for a verdict. The defendant's lawyer did not even renew his motion for a directed verdict. The jury found for the plaintiff for the full amount of the claim.

The defendant's lawyer has authority to decide whether to offer evidence for the defendant. If the defendant does not acquiesce, the lawyer still has the power to make the decision, and his action cannot be questioned at this time, as the judge in conducting an orderly trial will recognize the lawyer and accept his decision. Any objections which the defendant has may be presented later on a motion for a new trial, but the chance of this motion being granted is almost nil.

If the defendant's lawyer decides to put on evidence, he can now make an opening statement, assuming that he had not done so at the beginning of the trial. He will, as the affirmative lawyer did, tell the jury that, if he produces the evidence which he promises, he will expect a favorable verdict. He will then put on his evidence in the same manner that the affirmative put on its evidence.

Insanity has always been a complete common law defense to an accused person. There is a presumption that a person is sane, but once the accused offers some evidence of insanity the presumption falls, and the prosecution must prove sanity beyond a reasonable doubt. The prevailing test until recently was this: Was the accused so mentally impaired as not to be able to distinguish between right and wrong? If a jury found that he was mentally unable to make the distinction, he was acquitted as insane. This simple test is now being superceded in one state after another. The tests which are coming into effect are on a medical basis, whereas before the development of psychiatry they were on a conduct basis. One relatively new superceding test requires a jury to determine whether the crime was the product of a mental disease or defect. Mental disease or defect includes, as one court determined, any abnormal condition of the mind which substantially affects mental or emotional powers and substantially weakens control of behavior. The prosecution must show either absense of mental disease, or, if it was present, that it did not produce the crime.

Another superceding test being advanced is that a jury must determine whether the accused, as a result of mental disease or defect, lacked substantial capacity to know or appreciate the nature and quality of his act and, if he did know, was incapable of distinguishing right from wrong. As jurors are not qualified psychiatrists, they must weigh the opinions of psychiatrists plus those of lay witnesses. At first sight, the change of the sanity test to a mental health basis seems to be a boon to accused persons, since it offers the guilty a broader escape route than formerly. Sober thought, however, brings out the hazard of invoking the new basis for sanity. An accused who might otherwise expect a relatively short sentence may rely at trial on a defense of mental disease or defect, only to find himself in a mental institution for many years, perhaps for life.

So far, we have written of negative defense, but often there is an affirmative defense. In a civil case, the defendant may plead and undertake to prove a set-off, a counterclaim, a waiver, or contributary negligence. In a criminal case, the defendant cannot plead an affirmative defense; he is limited, in a case that goes to trial, to a plea of not guilty. He may, though, offer evidence of an affirmative nature, such as an alibi or self-defense as evidence of non-guilt, to weaken or destroy the state's evidence. He is, however, never under obligation to prove his innocence.

The great probability is that the evidence offered in behalf of the defendant will include some matters of fact about which the prosecutor's or the plaintiff's witnesses did not testify. Such matters should not be allowed to remain uncontradicted or unexplained. Consequently, the affirmative of the case is entitled at this point to offer evidence in rebuttal, contradicting or explaining any of the matters which have been introduced into the case by the defendant.

As an example, Jones sued Smith for damages to Jones's automobile caused by a collision of their two automobiles. Jones put in enough evidence to justify a verdict in his behalf. Smith, in defense, testified that after the accident he had a conversation by telephone with Jones and they agreed that each would drop his claim against the other, and each would pay for the repairs to his own automobile. This testimony, if allowed to stand uncontradicted, is sufficient to justify a verdict for Smith. Jones must rebut the conversation in some way or he will lose the case.

This opportunity to rebut the defendant's evidence is not the occasion for the introduction of new testimony to support the plaintiff's case. It is strictly an opportunity to offer evidence to contradict or explain—and thereby rebut—evidence, introduced by the defendant, which was not included in the plaintiff's case.

The end of the rebuttal marks the close of the taking of testimony, with one interesting exception in capital cases. At the common law, a defendant in a criminal case was not allowed to testify. This restriction seemed rather harsh in capital cases, so a practice was adopted to allow such a defendant an opportunity, at the end of the trial, to tell his story, without being put on his oath and without cross-examination. This gave him a chance to exculpate himself. This practice was a part of the common law in early American courts. Although such a defendant can now testify in his own behalf, the common law practice still is available. Accordingly, such a defendant can make an explanation, provided he has not testified. However, in this day, the exercise of this right would be extraordinary, since jurors will not be impressed by statements when the accused declines to testify under oath. Further, the accused's lawyer would hardly permit him to make a statement.

Decisions about the conduct of a trial often involve tactics. Some of the tactics do not meet with public approval. Indiscriminate use of them is one reason given by persons who are loath to be witnesses. They are not present in all trials, but are present often enough for the public to be aware of them and to fear their use. There are, of course, situations which justify almost any tactic which might produce truth; such instances are excused.

One tactic is knowingly to ask a leading question of one's own witness. It is quite the practice to initiate the examination of a witness by a few leading questions, such as name, address, and other matters not affecting the issue. An objectionable leading question is one regarding a material fact. Once the answer is given, it will, on objection, be stricken but the lawyer has gotten the answer voiced and expects that the jurors cannot obliterate the answer from their minds. This tactic is apt to backfire, as a keen juror will accept it as a sign of weakness.

Other tactics:

To restate the subject matter of a question which has been ruled out. The hope is that an answer will be given before the judge rules out the new question.

To make continual objections and arguments in the hope of diverting jury attention or diverting the witness. This tactic is particularly obnoxious when used at the time a crucial question is asked.

To ask improper questions in the hope that the opposing lawyer will make repeated objections and that these objections will create an impression in the minds of the jurors that the opposing lawyer is attempting to block full disclosure of facts about which the jury should be informed.

To attempt to center jury attention on some set of circumstances which are a side issue. This is the old red herring. Juries can be so diverted that they will decide a case on proof of issues that have nothing to do with the case.

To confuse a witness by asking, with an air of suspicion, whether he has talked about this case with anyone. If he had not, how could he be present at this trial? But many a witness thinks if he answers "Yes" it will somehow cost him face.

To misquote a witness, or misconstrue an answer, in the hope that the witness will not be sharp enough to make a correction.

To ask a series of questions to which a witness can readily

answer in the affirmative; then ask a question which the witness should answer in the negative, hoping that the witness is sufficiently confused to again answer affirmatively.

To prolong the time consumed in trial with the thought in mind that the longer the trial the larger the money verdict, or the better the chance to establish reasonable doubt.

10

Directed Verdicts

Now that the taking of evidence has come to an end, a break in the trial occurs in order to allow the lawyers to make and argue a motion that the judge direct the jury to render a verdict peremptorily, thereby bringing the trial to an end. In some states, this move is made by voicing to the judge a demurrer (exception) to the evidence; in some states, a motion is made to have the judge exclude all evidence; and, in other states, a motion is made for nonsuit. The practice in almost all state courts and in the federal courts is to make a motion for "a directed verdict." In many states, this motion must be made at this time in order to preserve the right to appeal the case.

The aim of this motion is to have the judge bring the trial, or some counts in the indictment or complaint, to a close by ordering the jury to render a verdict as ordered by him. Such an order, as to the whole case, comes as rather a shock to inexperienced jurors who had expected to deliberate on the evidence and reach a verdict. They wonder whether the judge has taken over tasks which are theirs—whether the judge has not, in fact, denied a jury trial. A large part of the public is also perplexed at this exercise of judicial authority.

We have made it clear that the prosecution must bear the burden of proof in a criminal case to prove a legal case beyond a reasonable doubt, and, in a civil case, the plaintiff must prove a legal case by a preponderance of the evidence. We also made it clear that a legal case is like the links of a chain. If all necessary links are not present, we do not have a chain; likewise, if all necessary elements are not proven, we do not have a legal case.

This motion for a directed verdict, when made by the defendant, in both criminal and civil cases, asserts that the evidence has not established all the elements necessary to make a case—the chain has a missing link. The question whether the evidence has established a case is a matter of law and not a matter of fact.

The authority of the judge to direct a verdict developed at the common law. It has always been held that this authority is incidental to, and flows from, the judicial function of determining the sufficiency of the evidence. Likewise, it has always been held that the right to a trial by jury does not extend to the right to a verdict *based* on jury deliberation.

The questions which the judge must consider in reaching a decision on this motion are: Do the facts brought out by admissible and substantial evidence and all proper inferences therefrom, considering all the evidence in the light most favorable to the defendant and ignoring all evidence to the contrary, establish a legal case? Do the facts so clearly fail to present a pertinent issue of fact that reasonable men, including jurors, could not disagree?

By substantial evidence is meant more than enough to give rise to a conjecture, a surmise, a suspicion, not entirely unreasonable, and not opposed to physical laws.

The judge usually excludes the jury from the courtroom while the lawyers argue these questions before him. If it appears that the arguments will be lengthy, the judge may excuse the jury for the rest of the day.

If the answer to either or both of the questions is in the negative, the judge can immediately take the case from the jury by directing the jury to render a specified verdict for the defendant. However, if there is a shadow of doubt in his mind, he can generally delay his ruling until after the jury has returned a verdict. This is a practical thing to do because, if the judge is later shown to be wrong in directing a verdict, or if an upper court reverses the case, it is not necessary to have another trial but only to reinstate the verdict. However, if it be clear that the motion should be granted or denied, the judge has a duty to grant it or deny it at this time.

Action on this motion is separate and apart from the functions of a jury and is in no way a usurpation of authority. The judge has found as a matter of law that there is no issue which calls for jury action.

If the judge grants the motion, he will order the jury to return a specified verdict. This is done without the jury leaving the courtroom. If any of the jurors refuse to render the desired verdict they can be held in contempt of court.

This, in general terms, is the essence of a motion for a directed verdict. The legislatures and the courts have specified some limitations and have made some distinctions in its use in civil and criminal cases. The more important of these need to be mentioned. Consider first who can make the motion.

In both types of cases the defendant can make the motion, and usually is the one who does so. In a civil case involving several counts, the result can be that certain counts can be stricken from jury consideration, or the entire case can be disposed of. Where there are multiple defendants, the motion can be granted to some and denied to others. In a criminal case, the jury can be ordered to find the accused not guilty on certain counts. Where there are more than one accused, the motion can be granted to some and denied to others.

The motion can also be made by the plaintiff or by the prosecutor. In a civil case, the motion can be granted on the basis that the defendant has produced no substantial evidence to support a defense. The jury would then determine the amount of damages to be awarded the plaintiff. It would be an extraordinary event for a defendant not to produce some defense; otherwise, there would be no occasion for him to incur the expense of trial. Yet it sometimes happens that cases are submitted to juries merely because the parties cannot agree on terms of settlement.

In a criminal case, as can be expected, the prosecutor is restricted. Some statutes preclude the prosecutor from making the motion in capital cases; some statutes preclude the motion in all cases involving felonies. Some states permit the motion in cases of misdemeanors where guilt is the only inference to be legally drawn. In Indiana and Maryland, where the jury passes on the law and the facts, the prosecutor is forbidden to make the motion.

Some state courts hold that nothing is more fundamental than that courts cannot instruct a jury to convict however clear may be the evidence of guilt. It is generally held that the judge may inform the jury of this limitation placed on him. The courts in other states hold that the judge can direct a verdict of guilt where the evidence is uncontradicted, clearly shows guilt, and there is no evidence of justification.

One question remains: If both sides make the motion, have both sides waived a jury trial and reposed the case with the judge? In civil cases, about half the states follow the New York rule which is that the case is taken from the jury by the consent of both parties. The other states hold the opposite view. In criminal cases, the authority of the prosecutor, as was stated, is restricted in various ways in various states. But in instances where it is possible for the prosecutor to make the motion, there is no harmony among the states as to the result when both sides make the motion. The lack of harmony makes it necessary to search the state law on this point.

If the motion is denied, the case naturally will proceed to a jury verdict. Jurors should not let themselves be influenced at all because the trial is allowed to continue. There is no basis on which jurors can reason why the case is allowed to proceed.

No authority exists that can compel a jury to bring in a verdict. One obdurate juror can hold out against the other eleven and cause a hung jury. When a jury cannot agree on a verdict, the foreman reports that fact to the judge. The judge's maximum authority is to instruct the jury along the lines of the "Allen Charge," which is set forth on page 193. The jury is then sent back to the jury room for further deliberations. If the jury again reports failure to reach a verdict, the jury should be discharged. If the judge pressures the jury to reach a verdict, the verdict is not a voluntary act, and, if an appeal is made, the verdict will be set aside. To meet the problem of hung juries some states provide that verdicts may be arrived at by less than unanimous vote. (See page 195.)

11

The Whole Truth

EACH witness takes an oath to tell the whole truth. No doubt it is expected that each witness, before he is excused, will have told the whole truth. Yet is any witness offered an opportunity to tell the whole truth? The witness is permitted only to answer questions. No one desires the witness to volunteer any testimony. The net result is that some witnesses who have valuable testimony are excused without having had an opportunity to give the valuable testimony.

The lawyers use a witness to testify as to facts which previously had been brought to the attention of the lawyer who calls the witness. The lawyer cannot be certain that the entire knowledge of the witness has been revealed to him. The lawyer will use the witness to testify to such of the previously disclosed facts as he desires to use. The cross-examiner may fortuitously bring out the whole truth, but he does not know it to be the whole truth. If this probability of limited disclosure is found in a willing witness, how much worse is it in connection with a witness who desires not to tell the whole truth?

A classic example to illustrate this is the story of the railroad crossing watchman who testified regarding an accident which occurred one night at the crossing when an engine struck a passenger car. He testified how he took his lantern out to the crossing and, as the engine approached, waved his lantern toward the oncoming automobile. After the trial he was asked if he was scared on the witness stand. He answered, "Yes, I was scared to death that I would be asked if the lantern was lit."

For our purpose, it can be assumed that there has been testimony favorable to both sides, and that there was a conflict in the testimony which created an issue of fact. A jury function is to resolve this conflict by weighing credible testimony. This requires jurors to determine what testimony is credible and what testimony is not credible.

This determination is often difficult. Consider that it requires a considerable period of contact with friends and acquaintances before we know what credit for truth and accuracy can be given to their statements regarding any matter in which they have even a cursory interest. An amazing amount of information which comes to us gratuitously is untrue or inaccurate. Yet jurors have only the short time during which a witness is giving testimony to form a tentative opinion of credibility. And this opinion is subject to change in the light of all the testimony.

All of us in our daily lives are the recipients of information which is sufficiently important to us that we must weigh its credibility. In the business world truth is so important that credibility of information must be determined. There are certain observations which we utilize almost daily to test truth. These are the same observations we use when we act as jurors. It seems worthwhile to outline some of these observations.

The strength of an impression tends to increase according to one's interst in the matter. One witness sees merely a piece of concrete. A concrete contractor will see a piece of concrete as having a four-to-one mixture.

Likewise, an impression is stronger when several senses are involved. So a person who merely saw a thing will recall less than one who not only saw but also felt and smelled the thing.

An impression is stronger when made in the absence of distractions. So a person in a position of danger and concerned with his own safety will record events less strongly than a person in a position of safety.

An impression is stronger when it is familiar. One witness sees only a truck. A truck dealer sees a truck of a certain make, style, and year.

The rapidity with which people can use their senses varies. As a well-known instance, crooked card deals are based on the fact that "the hand is quicker than the eye." Since people receive impressions under varying circumstances and into varying masses of mind matter, there is little cause to wonder that errors of reception are made.

Similar variations exist in the ability to call on memory or, as we say, to recall or recollect. One cannot at first recall a name, but if the name is mentioned, thus making the connection into memory, the witness recalls the name.

The mind tends quickly to reject the memory of unpleasant impressions. As we say of death, time is the only healer, for, in time, memory will become dim or absent.

Remember that the witness, while giving his testimony, is possessed of the traits common to all men. Note will be made of a few of these which consciously or unconsciously tend to sway the witness.

One fears to lose face; one tends to forget disagreeable facts; one tends to stick to a story once told; one dislikes to admit fault or error; one tends to place the blame on others; one's clan spirit makes him favor the side he is on; one favors the underdog.

A small percentage of people are romancers. To them, the truth has no meaning. There is no intent to lie; likewise, there is no intent to tell the truth. These people have minds which work very rapidly, and they have a way of letting the creative mind work without interruption, rather than interrupt the active mind and call on memory. There is no truth in them.

A witness who consciously lies about a sequence of events, in the expectation that he will be believed, undertakes a task greater than he realizes. If he succeeds in telling a consistently untrue line of testimony, he succeeds in concealing the true line as recorded in his memory. This in itself requires a high degree of mentality. The witness will, however, be concerned—and almost totally concerned—with words. Thereby he may dig his own grave.

There are three observable factors involved in consciously telling lies about a sequence of events. These are words, tone, and muscle reaction. Of the three, it is easiest to lie by word, harder to lie by tone, and hardest to lie by muscle reaction. In telling lies, while the words are being uttered, the mind will be checking for consistency, with a resultant slowing of the rate of speech. Under continual questioning, the witness may think that his lies are being detected, and, in order to cover up, will unconsciously increase his rate of speaking. In attempting to increase the speed of speech to a normal rate, he will err and speak faster than is normal. Respiration and circulation will be thrown out of normal, the witness will tend to perspire and will become generally uncertain in his attempts to control the flow of words.

The tone of voice, while lies are being told, will be a head tone, because the thoughts being voiced are the product of intellect. The tone of truth is related to chest tone. The muscles of the eye are almost impossible to control and, were they subject to control, it is doubtful if many witnesses would think to control them. Few people can keep their eyes normally focused while telling a false tale for the reason that few can concentrate on vision and concentrate on ideas at the same time. As the expression goes, "The lips say no, but the eyes say yes."

If a witness, in testifying, is reliving mentally the events about which he is testifying, his emotions should be in play to some extent, and the normal reaction of the muscles should take place, although the reaction may be checked so as to show no more than the start of a response. If the start occurs, the result of natural co-ordination between mind and muscles, we tend to be persuaded that the witness is in earnest. If, however, there is not this rudimentary muscle reaction, we can expect that the witness is not reliving events but is projecting in words a mental picture which is the product of his conscious mind.

A witness who answers the questions of both lawyers with equal courtesy, promptness, fullness, and directness is more likely to be telling the truth as he recollects it than the witness who testifies in the opposite manner.

In weighing the testimony of a woman, consider whether the subject matter is such as to involve her emotions. The greater the emotional involvement, the less her testimony should be credited. Tears are not evidence.

105

Very few witnesses are without some interest in the outcome of the case. Some will be openly interested parties; some may derive a benefit, and others, tending to favor the side which uses them, will attempt to be a helpful witness to that side, even though they feel no awareness of being partisan.

The parties to the suit have a paramount interest in the outcome of the trial. They have ample time to consider all aspects of the case. They in particular will tend to forget or ignore unpleasant events connected with the issue and substitute a sequence of more favorable events. It is reasonably possible that, between the time of the happening of the event and the time of the trial, parties can convince themselves of a course of conduct widely distorted from the truth.

Agents and employees have a personal interest in protecting themselves from blame which may adversely affect their employment. Consequently, their first statement to their employer will, as a rule, be shaded to relieve the employee from blame, or at least minimize blame. Having once made a statement they will, when called as a witness, adhere stubbornly to their original statement. It seems that when self-interest comes in conflict with truth, truth often comes out second best.

In many instances jurors need the assistance of experts in reaching conclusions about matters beyond the scope of their knowledge. The courts allow for assistance to be given by experts in the field of knowledge involved. This witness must establish that he is qualified sufficiently in his occupation, by study and experience, to be classed as an expert. In regard to all expert witnesses, it can be said that they will be more likely to find what is wanted by the party who calls them and less likely to find and expose conditions adverse to that party.

The testimony of police and other enforcement officers should be subject to scrutiny. These men are presumably interested in the preservation of order. A jury is likewise interested in the preservation of order. It seems, then, that all are on the same side. But this is not a guarantee that enforcement officers always tell the truth or, particularly, that they give the full truth. The pressure to make an arrest and to prosecute in answer to

106

public demand for action can influence testimony; there may also be personal reasons for not revealing all known facts. Enforcement officers have some degree of professional interest in the successful prosecution of accused persons.

These examples are pointed out to indicate the improbability that a witness, however good his intentions, has actually performed according to his oath to tell the truth, the whole truth, and nothing but the truth.

When a jury is convinced that a witness is a perjurer, it can ignore his testimony. It has no duty or authority to report a witness it finds to be a perjurer. Punishment for perjury is so infrequent that little threat hangs over the head of a perjurer.

It is remarkable that indoctrination of the western world for centuries with the Ninth Commandment, "Thou shalt not bear false witness," has produced such meager results.

➤➤ 12 ⧫⧫

. . . and in Closing

EACH lawyer now has the opportunity to address to the jury a summation of the evidence supporting his side of the case. The lawyer representing the affirmative (the burden of proof) sums up first. Then the defense lawyer sums up, after which the affirmative lawyer can make a rebuttal. The summations afford an opportunity for each to marshal the facts which each hopes will lead to a verdict in his favor.

Recall that each lawyer, in his opening statement (assuming that the defendant's lawyer made a statement), indicated what facts his side would prove, and that he would ask for a verdict in favor of his side. It is reasonable to expect that each will explain to the jury that he has done this and through what sequences of evidence he has done it, with the logical result that a verdict should be forthcoming in favor of his side. Then the lawyer would be regarded as an honest man who carries through his undertakings, and the inference is that his case is honest. Jurors anticipate that lawyers will do this, but, strange as it may seem, this course is not usually followed.

It is safe to say that outstanding advocates have at least three qualities in common. They have the capacity to make trivial statements in a manner which transforms them into statements of seeming magnitude; they are earthy men who have charm; and they are able to speak on the level of the jurors.

The advocate has little opportunity for persuasion in contract cases; he must convince rather than persuade. In tort trials and in criminal trials, the lawyers have broader scope. The difference in scope is due to the amount and force of the positive factor of sympathy, and the negative factors of prejudice and bias. Prejudice and bias are unpopular words and few men admit to either. Therefore, it will be better to include these and sympathy in the general field of emotions. All people admit that they have emotions.

Emotion dominates the actions of daily life. It is false to assume that jurors can bypass emotion and reach verdicts based solely on reason. An observation will make this clear. Reason dictates that all adults should build a nest egg against the rainy day to come, and should do this at a cost of depriving themselves of lesser needs. Will they act as reason dictates? A survey made in a large city disclosed that eighty per cent of the residents could not go thirty days without a paycheck. Eighty per cent of an enlightened community allowed the enticements of advertising, their desire for fulfillment, their vanity and other emotions to dominate so as to keep them in a precarious economic position. These people compose the veniremen to a great extent. Why expect them to act without the influence of emotion in the lone instance of jury service?

It seems, then, that as a practical matter the most that the law can expect from a juror is that he will not permit himself to be carried away by emotion, and that he will respect reason enough to keep it from being obliterated. Emotional factors can be and are used to affect verdicts. The jury system must and does work in this atmosphere. Lawyers, as a part of the system, work in this atmosphere.

Cases based in tort, wherein money damages are to be awarded, and cases in crime present an opportunity to lawyers to use emotion as an aid in obtaining large verdicts or a not-guilty verdict. A few examples of what the lawyer can do: Play on the assumption, accepted even if untrue, that the female is delicate, frail, and particularly sensitive to pain. Play up any element of beauty which she may have. Exaggerate her family devotion. In other words, fortify the emotional attitude of male jurors toward women. Play up reputed "frustrations" and "maladjustments." Play on "the stark facts of life with which plaintiff and the jurors do daily battle." Live with the jurors on the basis of the inane supposition "you know and I know." Use

109

the two old favorites—"father of a loving family" and "veteran of military service." Use incidental items of evidence to obscure the vital evidence. This type of argument reminds one of what H. L. Mencken called "sonorous nonsense driven home with gestures."

Incidental evidence can be used to get the jury off onto a bypath and away from harmful pertinent evidence. Take, as an illustration, the case of an employee accused of stealing from his employer. The employee's lawyer can lay such stress on the man's unduly low pay that the lawyer may lead a juror from the real issue of theft to the artificial issue of wage scale—and thereby put the employer on trial.

Lawyers realize that the American people have an overwhelming curiosity as to motive. They seem never to tire of reading mystery stories which depict a crime and then go on from page to page to show that several people have a motive which might induce them to commit the crime until finally one of them is disclosed as the criminal. The *motive* for a crime and the *intent* with which it is committed are not synonymous because, while motive may be the moving cause which induces action, intent is the purpose or design with which the crime is committed and is always an essential ingredient of crime. So a person may have a vile motive but no matter how vile the motive may be it is not criminal. Nor is laudable motive a legal excuse for crime.

However, it is proper at a trial to expose motives which might have induced the accused to commit the crime. The motive has great probative force in determining guilt, especially in cases based on circumstantial evidence, but there must be additional evidence in order to establish intent. Intent cannot be proven as a fact. This is necessarily true because no one can delve into the mind of an accused person and find intent. So, the law says that a person is presumed to intend the probable consequences of his acts. Legal intent may, therefore, be presumed, and, where supporting evidence establishes some basis for a finding of guilt, intent clinches a verdict of guilt.

Thus, it is proper for the prosecutor to argue that the motive is strong and for the defendant's lawyer to argue the absence of motive or the weakness of any motive brought out by the prosecutor. Motive alone cannot establish intent; it can establish only a basis for intent. At the same time, absence of motive fortifies reasonable doubt. It is, therefore, possible that a lawyer can direct attention away from intent and thereby persuade a jury to weigh guilt on the spurious defense of insufficiency of motive.

All this is not intended to give the impression that juries are swayed as willow trees. Neither is it intended to infer that all lawyers can sway jurors, that all jurors can be swayed, or that a juror will continue to be swayed. There is the sobering-up time while the judge instructs the jury on the law—and also the sobering effect of argument in the jury room by fellow jurors who have not had their emotions aroused.

There is no way to foretell what particular fact or circumstance will influence a juror. Many instances are known in which the persuasion came from something not touched upon by either lawyer in argument because neither thought the fact or circumstance was of importance. Consider this case. After a rear-end collision, a suit was filed by the owner of the struck car, and his wife. The suit claimed damages to his car and damage to the wife's nervous system, plus a few bruises. She was a strikingly good-looking young woman. It appeared that the wife's looks were counted on to induce a substantial award. After the accident, the wife was taken to a doctor's office nearby, not by her husband but by the other driver. It seemed that her husband stayed at the scene of the accident. He never did go to see the doctor. The jury found for the other driver. A juror later said, "That fellow wasn't interested enough in his wife to visit the doctor. We wouldn't give him a thing." Note that the juror made no reference to her injuries. (This verdict was so far off the mark that it was set aside. Later, the case was settled for car damage only.)

Many times a lawyer will realize that the evidence is all against him, that his case is hopeless. Yet he will address the jury and put forward the most favorable interpretation of the evidence that he can think up. A lawyer shows his courage by undertaking to argue such a case.

The practice of allowing liberality in the scope of argument is, in the long run, sound. The litigants hear their cases argued in the most favorable light by an advocate of their own choosing. The loser than feels that there has been no impediment to his case, that he has had a full and fair trial. He can take the loss in good, or at least in better, grace. The opportunity for both sides to make a full closing argument is one reason for public satisfaction with the jury trial system.

The Judge's Charge

THE public views conduct from the standpoint of morality, the question being: Was the conduct right or wrong? Courts are not concerned with morality but with law. With courts the question is: Was the conduct legal or illegal? If there is no ban by law, conduct is legal whether it be "right" or "wrong." *Wrong* is a matter of gradations depending on the moral status of individuals, and it is, therefore, indefinite. *Law,* whether it be common law or statute law, is specific and definite.

The moralist will say: "Thou shalt not steal." Law cannot operate on the basis of an indefinite word like "steal." Law prohibits, within the scope of stealing, definite acts, such as petit larceny, grand larceny, robbery, armed robbery, embezzlement, false pretenses, taken without right, and unauthorized use. Accordingly, an indictment or information must state a precise charge or charges. The defendant goes on trial solely on the specified charge or charges and no others.

On the civil side, one who holds the property of another by permission is called a bailee. The owner is called a bailor. The law says that a bailment must be viewed from one of three angles. Is it for the benefit of the bailor, is it for the benefit of the bailee, or is it for their mutual benefit? The obligation of the parties differs according to who gets the benefit.

A layman cannot be expected to know these and other particulars of criminal and civil law. In order, then, that a jury be enlightened, it was desirable, if not necessary, that jurors be told the applicable law. This enlightenment has been given by the judge since early times in what is called the charge (instruction) to the jury.

113

The common law, as previously stated, is based on following precedents. Each case that was tried dealt with some point of law and became a precedent to be followed in subsequent cases. Gradually, a body of cases accumulated, patterns of cases were established, and the law took definite form. Because it was desirable to have law uniform, the practice was established of having the judge state the law to the jury. This was particularly important, considering that the proportion of illiterate people at that time was very high. Juries were expected to accept and apply law as the judge stated it to be. By doing so, a jury makes principles of law applicable uniformly to all people and so affords equality under law.

In some states the judge is not required to charge the jury. Nevertheless, in these instances means are provided to get instruction of the law to the jury.

The instructions[1] will likely follow a pattern of four parts:

1. Explanation of the issues.
2. Explanation of the position taken by both sides.
3. The principles of evidence and their application.
4. The rule, or rules, of law which will be applicable to any factual situation which may be found in the evidence.

The judge may also give specific instructions particularly applicable to the case at trial, so that when his entire charge has been completed, it can be assumed that he has covered the points of law essential in the case. Generally, the judge will receive from the lawyers for the respective parties any instructions which they offer as applicable law in the case. The judge rules on the legality of such requested instructions and may permit the lawyers to read them to the juries, or he may incorporate them in his general charge.

The judge's charge to the jury can be the basis of an appeal to an appellate court on the claim, by the party taking the appeal, that the judge gave erroneous instructions to which the lawyer objected at the time of trial; or that the judge refused

[1] A few of the instructions frequently used are set forth under Instructions Applicable to Criminal and Civil Cases. (See page 188.)

114

to give certain instructions which the lawyer requested the judge to give. The great majority of appeals involve the question whether the trial judge properly instructed the jury as to the law.

A trial judge is not free to impose his personal idea of the controlling law. He is bound to follow law as established by the appellate courts of his state. The printed and bound decisions of the appellate courts will be examined by both lawyers and judge to try to determine whether the point of law has been previously decided. If the point has been decided by the upper court of his state, the decision constitutes a precedent which the judge is bound to follow, on his oath of office. The difficulty is that hardly any two cases are exactly alike, so it becomes necessary for the judge to decide whether the upper court has established a legal principle definitely applicable to the facts in the particular case at trial. To put that thought in other words, the judge questions whether, if the upper court had to decide the law on the facts of the case at trial, it would find the law controlled by a certain decision. If the answer is in the affirmative, he must follow the precedent. If there is no applicable precedent or no precedent which guides the judge's mind, a search is made for precedents in other states. These are not binding on the judge, but are useful guides. If this search reveals no precedent, the judge is left to his best resources. The result is that the judge then makes an effort to determine what the highest court would determine the law to be on the facts of the case at trial. This is the most difficult task the trial judge has to perform. Trial judges are not infallible in predicting what upper courts will decide if an appeal reaches them. They never know when a majority of the appeal judges may become a minority and reverse a former decision. Considering that opinions of Justices of the United States Supreme Court are so often split five to four as to the law, it is not surprising that the trial judge makes an occasional error in stating the law of the case.

These close decisions are particularly troublesome to trial judges because the later replacement of one judge may bring about a shift to a four–five situation. A five–four decision usually indicates that the applicable law is in a state of flux. The trial judge is thus often placed in a position of some degree of uncertainty when he instructs a jury.

The appellate courts presume that the jury heard and understood and acted on each and every word of each instruction. The presumption is of doubtful virtue, if indeed it has any virtue. It is, though, a necessity and may be classed as a necessary legal fiction. A few words too many in an instruction or a few words missing may be ruled as sufficient cause for reversal. Unfortunately, some decisions are of such nature and complexity that they require some instructions to be lengthy, legalistic, and perhaps confusing. The trial judge should not be blamed if his instructions at times are difficult for a jury to comprehend and are made to meet appellate approval rather than meet the understanding of laymen sitting as jurors. This problem can be met by the foreman's asking that such an instruction be restated in writing so that the jurors may study it during their deliberations.

The general rule is that the jury is required to accept and apply the law as instructed by the judge. No juror has the right to act according to his personal view of what the law is or should be. A juror is not acting as an individual, but as a trusted member of a group acting as a unit. If the judge is in error in his statement of the law, his error can be corrected on a motion for a new trial or on an appeal. On the other hand, if a jury acts contrary to instruction, correction is most difficult and may be impossible.

There is considerable misunderstanding in the minds of the general public regarding provisions making a jury the judge of fact and not of law. This misunderstanding is attributable in large part to the inaccuracy of the general rule that juries decide *only* the facts. This is an inaccurate expression because it leaves the impression that juries are not judges of the law at any time or in any sense. Juries are always judges of the law in the sense that juries must pass on the manner and the extent in which the law expounded by the judge fits the facts brought out in the evidence. This process requires juries to perform the legal function of interpretation and application.

116

In the absence of express authority, however, juries are not judges of the law in the sense of determining what principle of law is applicable to the evidence.

As an illustration of questions on which a judge instructs, consider this case: A man we'll call Walker is walking in an aisle of a national chain store and perhaps using the aisle as a shortcut between two streets. Walker is knocked down by another patron and breaks a leg. Investigation discloses that the patron was in an altercation with the store manager who pushed the patron into Walker, who sues the owner corporation. The judge must instruct the jury on the rights of Walker, the plaintiff. These rights depend on whether Walker was in the store as an invited customer, or as a person merely permitted to be there, or as a thief, or as a trespasser. Was the altercation between the patron and the manager a personal matter, or was it about some business of the store? If the manager had a right to use force, was the force he used excessive? Assume the manager acted wrongfully, what proof is necessary to hold the corporation liable? The judge charged the jury that, if it found Walker to be a customer, he was entitled to due care; that if it found that the altercation between the patron and the manager arose out of store business, the manager still was required to be careful about Walker, and if the manager was not careful, the owner would be liable.

When the judge relates the law to the facts, he always does so on the basis of an "if." He will say: "If you find the facts to be so and so then your verdict shall be so and so, but if you find the facts to be so and so your verdict shall be the opposite." This leaves the jury to decide the facts and reach the proper conclusion.

The general rule that the jury takes the law as instructed by the judge is subject to some exceptions. The constitutions of nineteen states provide that in trials for criminal libel the jury is judge of fact and law. If the words used in each constitution are not qualified, the judge instructs what the law is but his instructions in almost all states are advisory only and he will so state. In these instances the jury is under no obligation to follow

117

instructions. Most constitutions, however, qualify their references to jury power with such words as "under the direction of the court." These constitutional provisions were made under the special circumstances existing before the year 1776 to do away with fear of suppression of free speech or comment.

The constitutions of Indiana and Maryland provide that in criminal trials the jury shall be the judge of fact and law. These provisions are to be taken literally; any instruction by the judge is advisory only.

In Georgia, Louisiana, and Oregon, there are constitutional provisions giving juries apparent powers as judges of the law, at least in applying it. But the effect of these provisions is not contrary to the general rule that the jury take the law as instructed by the judge.

In Illinois, a section of the Criminal Code makes juries the judges of law and fact. This has been construed to mean that the judge has a duty to instruct, if requested, but the jurors are not bound if they can say that they know the law better. If the jurors find the judge is wrong on the law, the statute gives them that right.

These provisions are confusing, if not contradictory, for they seem to make a judge charge a jury by saying, in effect: "You, the jury, are by statute the judges of the law. But, by the same statute, you will accept my judgment as to what the law is."

It is only in the criminal trials in Indiana and Maryland, and in some other states in criminal libel trials, that juries are under no obligation to follow the law as it may be stated to them by the judges. In these instances, juries have not only the authorization to determine the law, but also are authorized to determine what construction of the law is applicable to the facts established by the evidence.

The judge will also include in his charge instructions about the proper form of a verdict. (Verdicts are discussed in Chapter 15.)

We cannot leave this subject without considering the authority of a trial judge to comment to the jury on his personal opinion of the credibility of witnesses and the weight of evidence. At the common law, the trial judge had the authority to do so, provided that he made clear to the jury that it was not bound in any way to accept his views, and that it was the sole judge of these matters. As all trials in federal courts must be as at the common law, federal judges do have this authority. The exercise of this authority did not always meet with public acceptance. It was thought that the imposing position of the judge, together with his broad experience with trials, gave such impact to his views that they unduly influenced jurors to accept his views. It was also thought that his comments impinged upon the jurors' right and duty to find the facts without influence, bias, or prejudice. At the same time, it was thought that some jurors might resent this seeming impingement as domineering and be influenced to take the opposite view. As a result, some state legislatures have denied to judges in their state courts the right to comment on the credibility of witnesses and on the weight of the evidence. In recognition of public opinion on this matter, other judges are loath to exercise this authority and seldom express their personal views.

⇛ 14 ⇚

Inside the Jury Room

WHEN the door of the jury conference room closes, the jury has the case. No person is allowed in the jury room. Up to this time the jurors have been spectators; now they become actors. The jurors know that they are about to perform a function of government; that they are participating in a trial system which their ancestors preserved for their use; that if they need a jury at some time in the future they can expect no greater concentration to duty than they now give; that their verdict is open to public knowledge and possible criticism; that the jury is a team and the team must perform well.

The first act of the jury is to select a foreman. In some states juror number one is the foreman. The foreman acts as presiding officer and as spokesman for the jury.

It might be well to set out here two wise comments regarding the attitude toward litigants on the part of judges and jurors.

Judge Jay, the first chief justice of the United States Supreme Court, said, "Justice is always the same, whether it be due from one man to a million, or from a million to one man."

Albert Jay Nock, one time editor of the *Atlantic Monthly,* said, "Justice is always the same in the case of men and things you do not like, as in the case of those you do like."

There is no prescribed form which jury deliberations must follow. There are, however, several things which a juror may not do. These are the principal ones: A juror must not play detective and seek evidence or clarification of evidence; he must not talk to anyone about the case outside the jury room until the trial is over; he must not allow others to talk to him about the case; he must avoid hearing others discuss the case; he must avoid newspaper stories and news reports about the trial; he must not allow strangers in the jury room. And, of course, he must stay with the other jurors, and he must stay sober. If a violation of any of these obligations is brought to the attention of the judge, he will weigh whether a party has been prejudiced by the violation. If he finds that a party has been prejudiced, he can discharge the jury or set aside its verdict.

The reading of newspaper reporters' accounts of the trial is the error which jurors are most apt to commit. A juror may be curious about whether his name is mentioned, or how much prominence is being given to the trial. However, it is not unusual that the news reporter, especially in criminal trials, has picked up and had printed prejudicial information which is not admissible in evidence. The judge determines whether the printed or radio account is prejudicial to the degree that a normal person would be influenced by it. If so, the juror who read or heard the account is presumed to have been influenced, and his value as an impartial juror is destroyed. The courts have no power to limit a free press in this regard. The only redress available to the court is to declare a mistrial.

Jury deliberation is the heart of the jury trial system. Every pertinent fact should be brought up by some juror and its credibility and importance weighed by all jurors. In a trial by judge, the evidence is acted upon by one man, who does not have the help of disinterested persons in exposing all facts, in drawing correct inferences, in examining the elements of credibility, and in weighing each item of evidence. Each juror, however, has the help of the other jurors.

A few suggestions can be made concerning the process of weighing evidence. It is hardly conceivable that any item of evidence can stand by itself without the support of other evidence. A revolver is offered in evidence as being the weapon used in committing the crime. The revolver is real evidence but before it can be admitted in evidence it must be properly identified as the weapon used in the crime. Oral testimony is neces-

121

sary to connect the revolver with the defendant. The jurors must pass on the credibility of this evidence, and will not assume that the revolver in evidence was the one used, unless they are satisfied beyond a reasonable doubt. If they are so satisfied, the revolver is accepted as truth.

Likewise, in a civil case, there was evidence that a skid mark was impressed on the pavement. The skid mark is real evidence. But testimony is required to establish that the particular skid mark was impressed by the defendant's automobile. The jury must pass on the credibility of the witnesses who connect the mark with the automobile. If the jury credits this testimony the mark is accepted as truth.

Once having examined the items of real evidence and accepted some as proven, or as truth, the jury can use the accepted items as the criteria with which all testimony must harmonize. So, if the skid mark indicates a speed of fifty miles per hour, no testimony of a lesser speed will receive any credit.

Usually there will be in a case items of evidence based on physical facts, or based on laws of nature. Testimony which is in accord with these solid truths will weigh heavily. On such a foundation of proven facts, a jury can progress to a sound verdict.

The initial question for a jury to decide is the guilt or liability of the defendant. Each juror can be expected to have tentative impressions which incline him one way or the other. Jury deliberations examine the force and validity of these impressions. For this reason, it is not wise for a juror to have—or to express—a fixed opinion before deliberation, for there is the danger that, having taken a position, he will tend to retain it. Nor is it advisable to take an immediate vote. Especially is this true in those states which, in civil cases, do not insist that a jury verdict be unanimous. These states allow verdicts by a certain number of jurors. The first vote can show that number in agreement, and this fact can shut off discussion. Full discussion might well result in a different verdict. It is far better to have discussion before any vote. If jurors will make statements on the evidence or the law with the limitation "As I see it now," each juror leaves his opinion open to change as the discussion leads to agreement. Each juror is free to change his early views to concur with the other jurors on the facts and the correct applicable law. The important thing is that the evidence, with all proper inferences, is the only thing that counts.

If the jury in a criminal case finds the defendant to be guilty, it proceeds to frame its verdict in accord with the instructions it received. In civil cases, if the verdict is in favor of plaintiff, the jury proceeds to determine the amount of money it will award. These are considered separately.

Statutes in some states authorize juries, in certain cases, to assess the penalty to be imposed on criminal defendants who are found guilty. Other states authorize juries to recommend the penalty or to recommend clemency. In these instances, juries do not consider laws under which terms of sentences may be reduced for good behavior, nor what a parole board may do in the future. These means of reducing the penalty are not part of the jury function.

Other than the limitations of sentence provided by law, a jury has no standard on which to base punishment. Jurors are not expected to know the social factors entering into sentencing. Jurors and judges mete out punishment based on how they evaluate a mass of intangibles. This fact is pointed out to focus attention on the lack of a scientific basis for punishment. It follows that a judge or jury sentence is largely dependent on the attitude of judge or jury to the nature of the crime, the circumstances of the crime, the apparent moral worth of defendant, and similar intangibles. One sentence will be based on a hard attitude toward criminals, and another sentence will be based on a soft attitude.

We will not be too far out of line if we make some observations on the subject of punishment for crime. In prehistoric days, men lived in tribes. A criminal was banished from the tribe. He was free all by himself to contend with the forces of nature—and he did not last long. This was an effective system so far as the tribe was concerned.

123

Our civilization has tried severe penalties such as cutting off hands, extracting tongues, stretching bodies on racks, whippings, hangings, and the horrors of Devil's Island, which was used by the French as a dumping ground for convicts. England handled the problem very nicely for a time by shipping convicts to America and Australia. After centuries of trial and error, we must admit that no satisfactory means have yet been found to rid ourselves of crime. Nor do we have proof that punishment set by the legislature or by a judge is preferable to punishment set by a jury. In frontier days the accused got summary sentence—most often a rope hung from a tree limb—yet crime persisted. Crime is with us always—we can but temporize with it.

In civil cases, a jury must determine the amount of award which will fairly compensate the plaintiff for the damage he suffered. Jurors have a relatively easy task in determining the compensation for physical damage; the compensation amounts to the value they place on property. Financial losses or business damages are fairly easy to determine. Here jurors deal with figures which are definite to a large degree.

The difficult jury problem is in reaching a fair award for such intangible items as pain and suffering, damage to reputation, loss of companionship, and the like. Each person suffers in a different degree. A football player will suffer a sprain, minimize the pain and make a quick recovery because he is intent on getting back into the game. An accident-conscious citizen who receives the same injury will have an entirely different response. There is no yardstick by which physical and mental pain can be measured. Each evaluation of pain and suffering is different. Jury awards for these items are not determined on a scientific basis.

Intangible factors include the jurors' valuation of a dollar, the defendant's apparent ability to pay, and the social and economic background of the parties and the jurors. When all the factors involved in determining awards for damages are considered, one can understand why awards greatly differ in similar cases. Some jurors will take a hard or strict attitude

124

towards the negligence of defendant; other jurors will take a hard attitude toward the exercise of care by plaintiff to avoid injury; still other jurors will take soft or liberal attitudes.

Obviously, a dominating factor in establishing the amount of the award for intangible damages is the ability of a plaintiff to describe the suffering in words which convey to the jury the validity and intensity of suffering. The ability to convey the reality and intensity of suffering is greater in women than in men. Women do not have inhibitions in describing their feelings. Men, on the other hand, are inhibited by a fear of being thought of as unmanly. This tends to make them shy and unable to explain their suffering fully.

As a general rule, the issues which a jury must decide are those which are the most difficult to decide. Civil cases in which the issues are not difficult should be settled out of court, or at least without a jury. In fact, it is necessary, in view of voluminous litigation, that the judges step in and make a sincere attempt to dispose of cases without trial through amicable compromise. Much is being done along this line, so that there is left for juries the hard core of civil cases. Likewise, in criminal cases a judge may accept a plea of guilty to a lesser offense than that charged if he feels that such action on his part does not jeopardize the interests of the community. The net result is that juries do not usually act in the run-of-the-mill cases, but do act when the parties have taken solid opposing positions on the issues.

If the issues were submitted to a judge, he would act without consultation with other people. If a two or three judge court tried the case, the judges would deliberate, but, being trained men, they are apt to take like views of conduct. They lack the common touch. Controversies are submitted to juries largely because they do have the common touch, because ultimate agreement requires that the evidence be scanned minutely, and because litigants desire that the verdicts be the result of full and fair deliberation by the entire jury. The success of the jury trial system depends on the sincerity of jury deliberations.

During deliberations, jurors may want to look at exhibits; to have parts of the testimony read from the transcript; to have further instructions on the law—or to obtain rest or refreshment. Word of any need should be sent to the judge through the jury custodian.

If the jury is in session at nightfall, permission may be given to conclude deliberations, deliver a sealed verdict to the custodian, and return the next morning when the verdict is opened. The jury may be permitted to go home and resume deliberations in the morning, or the jury may be locked up in some hotel for the night so the jury cannot be exposed to communications, tampering, or outside influences.

Discussion of jury deliberation might stop at this point. However, information on how a jury does or should deliberate will seem inadequate to some people, as it covers merely the objective aspects. They desire some light on the subjective aspects.

Jurors are not to allow emotional factors to produce a verdict differing from what the verdict would be if emotional factors were not present. It is not a function of the judge to give instruction on the why and wherefore of emotion, nor is there time for him to do so. It then seems necessary to briefly explain the brain as the source in the operation of emotion.

The human brain is regarded as the ultimate of creation. It is the object of ceaseless scientific investigation. Investigations to date have resulted in certain findings which are applicable here. We will consider the brain in two parts, the lower and the upper, and pass over the third or connecting brain. The lower brain, situated at the base of the skull, is the original or old brain with which man started his mental development. Studies have established that this brain has not changed in size or function, and that it is the source of all emotions. Studies have also established that emotions are associated with the two basic laws of nature: self-preservation and self-perpetuation. They are the driving forces in life, without which we would be inert. When emotional drive functions in approved channels, we have order and success. When it functions in other channels, we have disorder and failure.

The upper or new brain is the seat of thinking and reasoning. Man is the sole animal to develop this brain to a high degree. His skull has adjusted in size and form to permit the new brain to exceed the old brain in mass. One of the functions of this brain is to act as counsellor to and guardian of the old brain. It has capability to control the lower brain. Men differ, in that the respective drive of each emotion varies and in that the respective capacity to counsel and control each emotion varies.

Emotions seem to exist in opposites, such as affection and hate, aggression and fear. An animal may have fear to the extent of "freezing," but otherwise it has a split-second to decide to run or to fight. Once given to action, it will not reverse its course. In men, decision usually is delayed while the upper mind is consulted. Acts may be premeditated over a long period of time. On the other hand, a sudden emotion can trigger action so quickly that the upper mind has no time to act. The most obvious emotion is anger. One sees instances of accumulation of anger like a gathering storm or sees it as a burst of fury like a stroke of lightning. A study of anger in action—as we observe it in operation in our friends—will give an understanding of how emotions originate and motivate.

The law does not expect or require people to possess superior minds which can completely control emotions. It does require that degree of control or discipline possessed by the average man. A lesser degree of control can bring a penalty. The penalties set by law are adequate to deter the average man from wrongful conduct, but they are inadequate to deter people who, unwilling or unable to meet the minimum standard of control, become habitual criminals. In an attempt to deter such criminals, at least six states have legislation dealing with habitual criminals whereby the penalty is increased for second, third, and fourth convictions. In New York, it is mandatory that the penalty for a fourth conviction of a felony (other than murder and treason) shall be an indeterminate sentence with a minimum of not less than fifteen years and a maximum of life.

People like to pride themselves on possession of intellect and tend to delude themselves that their actions are governed by intellect. They seek to deny that the lower brain initiates action and that the upper brain merely directs or controls. There is no delusion, however, in the field of advertising. In other decades, advertisers told of the virtues of their products. That approach is good but the fact that a person is convinced of the merit of a product will not result in a sale. Modern advertisers seek, by illustration and allure, to produce an emotional reaction which will drive a person to buy a particular product.

The same principle applies to all situations where one person seeks to induce another person to take a definite action. Litigants desire to induce jurors to take definite action. They cannot do so merely by exclusive appeal to intellect; they must aim for the emotional drives of jurors. As in advertising, the evidence is not enough. Emotional appeal is a decisive factor. No verdict can be reached free from emotional involvement.

It is interesting to know how a jury works out a sympathy verdict. This case will illustrate the process. A man was standing in the street with the hood of his automobile up while he bent over and tried to make some minor repair. As he drew out from under the hood, he was hit by an automobile which was passing. There was no warning to the operator of the passing car. The injuries suffered by the plaintiff included fractures of the pelvis on both sides. If he got a favorable verdict, after the judge instructed that contributory negligence by the plaintiff would bar recovery, it should have been for at least ten thousand dollars. The jury brought in a verdict for only twenty-five hundred dollars. The defendant's lawyer later asked one of the jurors how the jury had arrived at the amount. The juror replied that the jury wanted to give a small verdict to the plaintiff, and decided that a verdict for twenty-five hundred dollars was the lowest that could stand up on appeal.

As there cannot be a jury trial free from emotional factors, it is not improper for litigants and lawyers to direct evidence to produce emotional appeal. This direction can be to little things, such as having all witnesses appear clean and neat. It can be to big things, such as building the love of a husband

128

for his wife, where the defense does in fact rest on "the unwritten law," a law which is not a legal defense.

The courts are not vigilant in requiring lawyers and witnesses to divest themselves of organization insignia in the form of lapel buttons and badges. These insignia can be downright influential. If objection to them is made, the wearer will be ordered to remove them.

Exhibits carry emotional appeal. For example, the bloody garments of a victim or the X-rays of broken bones. These exhibits can properly be the basis of argument by the lawyers in their closing summations. The closer appeals come to basic emotions the greater their force and effect. One side may use love of family to ameliorate crime; the other side may use hate in an attempt to explain vicious, brutal conduct.

Trials may also be affected by superstition. This is so subtle that it cannot be appraised. Nevertheless, it is recognized as a force. Consider that the United States Court House in Washington, D.C., has nineteen trial court rooms. Room No. 13 existed until it was changed to Room No. 12½—and then permanently to Room No. 21—because litigants did not want their cases tried in Room No. 13. No such change would be considered for Rooms Nos. 7 and 11.

Witnesses who testify to events cannot help but carry jurors along in vicarious participation, much as actors carry the audience along in an excellent stage play. Lawyers attempt the same thing in their orations.

Let it be admitted that a juror is bathed in emotion. Let it also be admitted that without the emotional aspects jurors would not be so willing to serve.

The mere fact that a case gets as far as the jury room establishes that there is at least one issue of fact for the jury to decide. This decision requires the acceptance of the viewpoint of the facts as sought by one side or the other. Each side, on the same facts, asserts that its viewpoint should prevail. The juror looks to the testimony to decide. The testimony did not come to him in written form; that is, in static form. The testimony came to him in dynamic form. The testimony and argument came from persons expressing emotions. The words used by a witness are charged with emotional force, which affects the emotional balance in the juror's mind. When these emotional forces enter a receptive mind, they bring into effect the corresponding emotional forces in the juror's mind. If the forces harmonize, the witness or lawyer has aided his side. When the forces do not coincide, the witness or lawyer has not aided his side. The juror, after weighing the favorable against the unfavorable, reaches a verdict. A jury decides on evidence, plus the emotional force of the testimony and arguments.

Any witness may tell a story that is unshakeable on cross-examination. A person *reading* the story would have no cause to question its truth. However, one juror receives the story, loaded with emotion, into a mind reacting emotionally. He may find persuasive reason to reject the story as basically untrue. He may feel that a single fact is missing. Another juror may receive the story with opposite emotional reaction and give full credit to the story. The two jurors then analyze the impulses which prompted each to make his initial response. They may then reach agreement. However, it can happen that the case has aroused a basic emotion in a juror which no process of reasoning will ever change. He will hang a jury by his lone vote. We observe this mental condition at times in girls who fall in love with truly worthless characters. The most substantial appeals to their upper brain fail to still the driving force of the basic emotion to mate.

Other matters in a juror's upper mind also affect the workings of his mind toward decisions. One item is particularly important—moral attitude. The minds of people in the western world are, in the main, dominated by Judean-Christian teachings. These teachings are based on the principle that the individual has the responsibility to learn and apply the law of the Divine Will. The observance of the laws of personal responsibility requires mastery over the lower brain. Violation by will or by carelessness, it is taught, brings retribution. A juror educated in the Judean-Christian tradition may be expected to act on the basis that a violation of law requires a sure finding of guilt without man-made excuses. This attitude tends to make a juror a rigid disciplinarian.

However, such is not necessarily the fact, because of two other Judean-Christian concepts which, right or wrong, also bear on the mind of a juror. The first concept is that man has a nature described as sinful. This concept can be used as a ready excuse for violation of law. It can be used to prompt a juror to reason that the law requires too much of such a weak creature as the litigant. A juror may call on the statement, "There, but for the Grace of God, go I." The other concept is that in daily life a person must show compassion. These two concepts tend to make a juror "soft." They also account for the desire of jurors to know the penalty which will follow a verdict of guilty.

A juror, then, must contend with his own emotional response to evidence—and with the emotional emissions from witnesses and lawyers. A verdict, thus, is the joint product of evidence plus emotional responses to evidence on the part of each juror. The same processes are at work in the mind of a judge when he decides cases without a jury. A jury trial offers an average response from several men, rather than a response from an individual.

Lest this discussion of emotion lead to confusion, it is well to return to the jury problem. In a civil case, jurors deal with persuasion; in a criminal case they deal with conviction. When jurors form a belief that a thing is so, based on total observation, reasoning, and emotion, yet concede the possibility that it might not be so, they can say, "I am persuaded." When they form an opinion that a thing is so and are unable to develop the possibility of its not being so, they can say, "I am convinced." The fact that these conclusions are based on facts which are weighed within the field of emotions does not preclude jurors from being honestly persuaded or honestly convinced. Society desires verdicts based on such honesty.

A splendid moving picture entitled "Twelve Angry Men" was based on jury deliberations. Eleven jurors were for conviction at the start of deliberations. This was the emotional response.

One juror, in the face of pressure from the other eleven, insisted on an examination of the facts. As he explained the shortcomings of the evidence of guilt, he got the eleven to shift from an emotional basis to a reasoning basis, and, in the end, the verdict was not guilty.

The jury trial system has undoubtedly had a great, though unmeasured effect on the development of political harmony in the United States. In the course of each year, about two million people sit as jurors. People, outside of jury duty, have little occasion to look objectively on the problems of their fellows. Nor have they been required to make binding objective decisions about the propriety of the activities of their fellows. Nor do people discuss objectively issues of conduct and reach decisions based on all available facts. The give and take of jury discussion exposes the thoughts of other jurors, from all classes of society and from all walks of life. From this comes a broader understanding of people's motives and conduct, and leads to community harmony.

»» 15 ««

The Verdict

AFTER a verdict has been reached, it is necessary to determine how to report it. A second trial and much confusion may be avoided if the verdict is not returned until the jury is positively certain that it is in a form which complies with the instructions given by the judge. If the jury is not certain how to report the verdict, the foreman should ask the custodian to arrange for a conference with the judge to make certain that it is in the correct form. When the verdict is ready, the foreman should notify the custodian that a verdict has been reached. When the judge and the lawyers are ready, the custodian will lead the way into the courtroom. The foreman will then render the verdict.

It is the privilege of the lawyer for the losing party to request that the jury be polled, that is, that each juror separately report his verdict. The clerk of the court will in that case call each name and ask each juror for his individual verdict. If all render the same verdict, that verdict will be accepted. If any one juror gives a verdict contrary to that announced by the foreman, the judge will send the jury back to the jury room for further deliberation.

The rendering of a verdict may appear simple but it is surprising how often the verdict is incomplete or improper in form. Erroneous verdicts are a pain to judges and litigants. Too much stress cannot be given to this point.

In one instance a plaintiff, a passenger in an automobile, sued the operators of the two vehicles which were in a collision in a state where proportionate damages are not allowed. The judge charged the jurors that if they found that both

133

operators were negligent they should bring in a single verdict against both for the damages. The jurors did arrive at an amount of damages. But they then went further and stated that they held that one defendant should pay three-fifths and the other two-fifths. The judge, who apparently did not like the low award for damages, immediately set the verdict aside. The case was later settled by one defendant paying twice the amount of the jury award.

In a state which permits verdicts on less than unanimous action, the jurors should be sure that the verdict *has been* reached by the required number, and that all who vote pro will be prepared to answer correctly if the jury is polled. The jurors also should make certain that all claims or charges subject to verdict are included in the verdict, and that they are consistent.

In criminal cases, the jury may be required not only to render a verdict as to guilt but, if the verdict is guilty, may also be required to go further and set the penalty within the limits allowed, or make recommendations as to the penalty.

In civil cases, the routine verdict is called a general verdict. This is relatively simple in cases wherein one party sues another. But, where the claims and the parties are multiple, each must be considered and properly related.

The modern trend in court procedure is toward making disposition of all claims arising from one event in one trial. There may be multiple plaintiffs who hold joint or individual claims; there may be multiple defendants charged with full or part liability for the event; there may be set-offs, counterclaims and cross-claims; there may be additional plaintiffs or additional defendants.

In a civil case, the jury may be required to return a special verdict. Such verdicts have an historical background. It was pointed out earlier that, at the common law beginning of jury trials, if a jury verdict by twenty-four was contrary to a general verdict of the initial jury of twelve, the initial twelve were subject to attaint. This penalty could be avoided by a jury's returning a special verdict limited to findings on the material issues of fact and leaving to the judge the application of the law and the determination of the verdict. Jurors once preferred to give special verdicts, but this is no longer true, since there is no longer any reason to fear attaint. Special verdicts were also used in cases where the issues were "of too great nicety for the discussion of ordinary freemen," and they are used today in many courts for the same reason.

In most states, when the trial judge believes that the issues of fact are too numerous or complex for the average man to keep clearly in mind, he may order the jury to bring in a special verdict. He may direct the jury to bring in a verdict based on answers to his stated questions on the issues of fact. There must be harmony between the answers and the verdict. Otherwise the judge can send the jurors back to see if they can harmonize the verdict with the answers.

When the verdict is accepted by the judge, the trial is at an end. The jury is then discharged.

State courts are not in harmony as to whether a judge can require jurors to answer questions after a verdict has been rendered and before the jury is discharged. The law in many states has not been established. Some few states hold that a juror cannot be questioned. Others hold that, under his general supervisory power, the judge can question the jurors to ascertain whether the verdict was arrived at by mistake or was based on misapprehension, and also to ascertain whether there has been misconduct on the part of any juror.

One example of very simple confusion occurred when, on the return of the jury, the clerk asked, "For whom is your verdict?" The foreman answered, "For the defendant." There was then a commotion among the jurors, and some jurors pulled the tail of the foreman's coat. The judge, noting the commotion, said, "You had better retire because you seem in disagreement." The jury marched out of the courtroom—and came right in again. Then the verdict was announced: "For the plaintiff."

After the jury is discharged, the jurors are free to talk to anyone about any aspect of the trial, unless they have agreed that no juror will talk about the case. It is probable that the lawyers will seek to learn the basis of the verdict. Disclosures made by jurors may contain some fact which will give the losing party a basis for moving to have the verdict set aside. A wise juror will be cautious in explaining a verdict.

As far as the jurors are concerned, the case is now closed. But it may not actually be closed. In a civil case, the losing party can move for a new trial, and if that motion is denied, he can appeal to the next higher court on claimed errors of law. In a criminal trial ending in acquittal, the case is closed. If there is a conviction, the defendant can move for a new trial, and if that is denied, he can file an appeal on claimed errors. Since the prosecution cannot appeal a criminal case, the accused gets the benefit of any error committed during the trial.

A unique situation exists in Connecticut. The Fifth Amendment to the Constitution of the United States provides, among other things; "nor shall any person be subject for the same offense to be twice put in jeopardy of life or limb." This seemed to be ample support for the conclusion that the prosecution cannot appeal a criminal case. Further support is in the understanding of the people of the United States that this is a basic principle. But the state of Connecticut upset that conclusion.[1] That state enacted a statute providing: "Appeals from the rulings and decisions of the supreme court or of any court of common pleas, upon all questions of law arising on the trial of criminal cases, may be taken by the state, with the permission of the presiding judge, to the supreme court of errors, in the same manner and to the same effect as if made by the accused."

The defendant, having been charged with first degree murder, had been convicted of second degree murder and was sentenced to life imprisonment. The state appealed the case on the authority of the statute just cited.

On retrial, the defendant was convicted of first degree murder—and sentenced to death. He appealed all the way to the

[1] Palko v. Connecticut, 302 U.S. 319 (1937).

United States Supreme Court. That court affirmed the second conviction saying: "The state is not attempting to wear the accused out by a multitude of cases with accumulated trials. It asks no more than this, that the case against him shall go on until there shall be a trial free from the corrosion of substantial error." The court is not saying that a man can be twice put in jeopardy. The innovation is that the court says that a state has the right to determine when the first jeopardy has terminated.

At any time up to the conclusion of taking evidence, a mistrial could have occurred. It sometimes happens that a question which is improper under the rules of evidence, or an answer to a question, or an act in the presence of the jury, is so prejudicial to a litigant that the judge believes that the prejudicial effect cannot be overcome by admonishing the jury to ignore the matter. The litigant is prejudiced beyond remedy. In such an event, the judge will state to the jury that he declares a mistrial. The jury is then dismissed and the case is set over for retrial at a future date, with, of course, a new jury.

A mistrial also can be declared on account of prejudicial statements made in final arguments, misconduct of a juror, prejudicial outbursts from spectators, and other unexpected prejudicial events which jurors cannot be expected to ignore.

Mistrials are few and far between. This is a surprising fact when we consider the temptation to bring them about. A party who becomes aware that his case has taken an unfavorable turn due to failure of witnesses to appear, failure of witnesses to testify as expected, failure to have proof available to meet unforeseen damaging evidence—and like causes—will be benefited by a mistrial. He may do better on a retrial. This prospective benefit constitutes a temptation to bring about a mistrial. Although the party, his lawyer, or both, may be held in contempt of court for attempting to bring about a mistrial, it is difficult to prove intentional misconduct.

A mistrial may be brought about deliberately by a juror who is sitting in a case which is distasteful to him.

A mistrial may also be brought about by a judge who may be aware that he has by some word or act made reversal possible if the verdict is appealed. For instance, there may have been a very sharp exchange of words between a lawyer and the judge in the course of which the judge said something highly prejudicial. As soon as a judge realizes that he has made an error that will later subject him to embarrassment when the case is reviewed in a higher court, the judge will, in all probability, be willing to entertain a motion for mistrial— on practically any grounds.

It is a tribute to the ethical standards of participants in trials that mistrials occur so seldom.

16

Jury Power

FROM the foregoing pages one might well conclude that no fundamental difference exists between trial by judge and trial by jury; that the two trial methods are merely elective on a basis of preference as to whether the facts in a trial should be determined by judge or jury; and that the right to jury trial is preserved for use whenever judges cannot be trusted or relied upon intelligently and truly to find the facts. If this were true, our forefathers in framing our constitutions were at great pains over a matter not justifying such precaution, and a matter which could have been cared for by providing an easy method for the removal of any venal, biased, or incompetent judge.

The fundamental difference in the two trial methods has not as yet been emphasized because at no place in the text was it necessary or proper to allude to the two usages of the word "justice."

One usage is, as previously stated, legal justice granted to the people by the Third Article and the first nine Amendments to the Constitution of the United States. This legal justice or, as we might say, constitutional justice, includes the right to a jury trial in both criminal and civil cases in federal courts. Jury trials are likewise provided for in state constitutions. In these trials another usage of the word justice applies. In this setting justice has the meaning intended to be conveyed in everyday use of the word.

Nowhere in our constitutions or statutes will we find a definition of everyday justice. Such justice cannot be adequately defined. It cannot be measured or standardized because it is a concept in the mind of each person and varies in each person.

It is synonymous with equity and morality. The sense of the word is inherent in each person. Each of us possesses a "sense of justice." We recognize it as a motivating force in our everyday actions.

There is no basis for an expectation that the sense of justice possessed by any one person is or can be just the same as the collective sense of justice arrived at by twelve jurors after deliberation on all the facts, circumstances, and motivations disclosed in a trial. It is reasonable to expect that the sense of justice in the mind of a judge will differ from that applied by a jury.

People who are raised in the same or similar environment tend to have a similar sense of justice, at least sufficiently similar so that we come to realize that there is in our community a level or measurement of justice expected by every person from every person. We know that the level changes from time to time; that what seemed just a century ago may not seem just today. We cannot be certain that what seems just today will be accepted as just a century from now.

The level of justice in a community is affected by the degree of acceptance of the authority of divine or natural law; by the proportion of people who hold that a force outside themselves works within them as a continual guide to thought and conduct.

The level of community justice is not based on the degree of justice exercised by each individual, but rather is based on an intangible concept which is possessed by each person irrespective of the justice of his individual conduct. So the level of community justice tends to be higher than the level observed by the members of the community in daily use.

Regardless of the difficulty of defining or explaining this community sense of justice, we know that it exists and we deal with the manifestation of it as a reality. For want of a descriptive word to express the idea of the community's collective sense of justice, it will be referred to as community justice. It is the standard which the community desires to be applied by the legislatures and by the courts.

The application of community justice in the formulation and execution of law may, at first view, seem simple, but in fact so many tangible and intangible factors exist that application is a complex problem.

It is a recognized fact that circumstances alter cases. It is impossible that lawmakers, past, present, and future, can have in mind all of the circumstances under which a law may be applied. In order to be definite and understandable a law cannot embody exceptions to cover all situations. Of necessity, the law, to be understood by laymen, must be definite, concise and expressed for specific application. It might be spoken of as static and inflexible. When statutes are made to cover situations with precision, we get such enactments as many provisions of the income tax laws, which even experts find difficult to understand. Law does provide degrees of offenses, and attempts by subdivisions to exercise justice by making appropriate penalty according to the severity of the offense, but it cannot make the innumerable subdivisions necessary to make the application of justice fit the particular circumstances of each case. For instance, the law does provide that a slayer shall not suffer penalty if he kills in self-defense or if he is of unsound mind. But the law does not provide relief for a slayer who kills under a degree of provocation that community justice might hold to warrant freedom from penalty, or to warrant a less severe penalty than that prescribed by law.

There can, therefore, arise instances, in the strict application of static and inflexible law, which offend the community sense of justice. Such, it is recognized, should not be so. Nor can it be said that lawmakers intended or desired it to be so. Lawmakers act in the knowledge that three means exist for the exercise of elasticity and flexibility in the application of law. The first is that the law may be amended to overcome an application contrary to public acceptance. The second is discretion exercised by enforcement officers in making arrests and prosecutions. The third is the exercise of discretion by jurors. If the second or third means is used, application of law is not in exact conformity with the law as written. However, such application makes the law, as written, practical and workable.

We deal here with the third means, that is, with the exercise of sound discretion by jurors. Such discretion is at the heart of the jury trial system. Understanding of the basis for the exercise of this discretion is essential to an understanding and appreciation of the system.

A jury is supposed to represent a true cross-section of the community, and the consensus of its members as to the definition and application of justice is, in theory, presumed to be that of the consensus of the community. A jury, then, possesses within itself that measure of justice which is community justice.

When a jury has under consideration a case in which a strict application of law to the facts calls for a verdict which will violate a juror's sense of justice, a direct conflict exists between law and justice. This conflict puts the law itself on trial. The conflict requires the jury to reconcile the conflict, that is, to make a choice between *law* and *justice*. At a recent trial, the judge charged the jurors that if they found the facts to be so-and-so their verdict should be murder in the first degree. The jury did find the facts so-and-so, but eleven jurors would not vote for a verdict except for manslaughter, which they felt was the correct degree of murder, since the killing had been committed in the course of a carousal. One juror insisted that the judge's instruction had to be carried out. However, he finally yielded to persuasion, and a verdict of manslaughter was returned. The judge then said to the accused's lawyer: "Don't ask for clemency for your client. The jury has already shown all the clemency he is entitled to."

As previously stated, jurors are generally instructed as to the law and instructed that they must follow the law as stated by the judge. However, jurors are not instructed as to justice or the presence of a conflict of law and justice; nor are they told how to resolve this conflict. It is difficult to reconcile this silence with the definition of courts as places wherein justice is judicially administered. Mention of justice in a trial is regarded as unnecessary because the courts have adopted a presumption that justice, as well as divine law, is worked into the fabric of the common law and the statute law. Jurors must reconcile the conflict in the circumstances of each case at trial. The thought has been expressed that jurors must bring the law down from the realm of theory to live with men. And thus jurors provide the elasticity which makes law livable and its operation satisfactory to the community.

A juror can accept this presumption regarding justice being woven into law for general application, but at times he may feel that justice is not incorporated in the law as applied to the particular case at trial. He recognizes the desirability of the law as written and yet cannot of his free will apply it in the circumstances. This leads naturally to an assumption by the juror that, had the lawmakers had in mind a set of circumstances such as in the case at trial, an exception might have been provided. This further leads to the thought that all exceptions cannot be foreseen, and, even though foreseen, it might not be practical to include them and add such volume to the statute law. The juror next asks himself: Is there, then, no room for an exception in the circumstances at trial, or is it left to me to make and apply an exception? Surely, he thinks, a court would not attempt to use him as an instrument to effect injustice.

He and all other people agree that there should be some elasticity in law, some opening through which community justice can enter, when necessary, to temper the cold, uniform application of law. There is basis for the thought that, if law cannot be applied with community justice, law must yield to community justice. If, then, a juror applies to a case this degree of justice, rather than the letter of the law, he feels that he has done right.

Jurors find themselves unable to function on the basis that trials deal merely with legality, to the exclusion of morality, which includes justice. When verdicts are rendered which do not appear to be based on strictly legal grounds, it may be enlightening to consider whether the jury has tempered law with community justice.

Two questions then arise. Do juries have the power to apply

143

their concept of community justice? Do juries have a legal right to exercise this power? The answer to the first question is an unequivocable affirmative. A jury has the power to bring in any verdict it desires. The verdict will stand, provided there is any credible testimony to support it. The outstanding case in which a jury refused to follow the law as contained in the instruction given by the judge is the historic Zenger case noted earlier. The judge instructed the jury to bring in a special verdict finding whether the libel had been published, and he would apply the law and determine guilt or innocence. Instead, the jury brought in a general verdict of not guilty.

Juries are protected in the exercise of this power. The constitutions of the colonial states prohibited use of the ancient writ of attaint—the right to punish jurors for failing to apply the law as charged. This principle was already embodied in law for, as previously stated, ever since 1670 a juror could not be punished for acquitting in the face of overwhelming evidence of guilt. Jurors are further protected in that a jury cannot be required by the trial judge to state reasons to support its verdict or be questioned as to how the verdict was reached. This broad statement may be subject to question in one or two states, but in them a judge would be most reluctant to question a jury.

Three procedural elements also protect jury power. One is that the judge's charge is based on "if you find." Who is to know which side of the "if" was accepted? The second is that the law assumes that the jury did accept the law as stated, except in flagrant instances. The third is that the law applied by the jury is not disclosed in the record, so the trial judge does not know, in the run of cases, whether his instruction was adopted.

The exercise of jury power is the only way in which the principle of community justice can be fully applied.

A judge is handicapped in any attempt to exercise community justice. In the first place, his entire training is to weigh conduct by the standard of legality. His oath of office demands that he use this standard. There is no public desire, demand, or expectation that he do otherwise. In fact, the demand is that he use the standard of legality. In many states, a judge is required to make findings of fact. His decision, then, is comparable to a special verdict. His findings of fact are assumed by all to be based on credible evidence. Neither lawyers nor appellate courts will accept a sense of community justice as a basis for a judicial conclusion.

A third handicap is that the judge is precluded from varying from appellate decisions. This may work for order, but it may not be fair to the judge. He, perhaps much against his will, will faithfully apply to his findings the previous decisions of the appellate court without any surety that the appellate court will not, in the future, reverse itself.

It is impossible to know the strength of a judge's desire to apply community justice and to what extent legalistic handicaps deter him. The factors which lead a judge to make a particular finding of fact may be conscious, subconscious, or unconscious. He may not truly realize all the factors which lead him to reach a particular finding of fact. His decision may turn on magnifying one finding of fact and minimizing others. In retrospect, it might be asked: Did the judge form his opinion before he found the fact? Was the fact found to conform to the formed opinion?

A trial judge is well nigh precluded from applying justice except in two instances. In criminal cases, penalties, usually imposed as a judicial function, can be determined in accord with the judge's concept of justice in the light of the evidence. In civil cases involving application of law which has not been definitely fixed by statute or by a decision of the appellate court, the trial judge has leeway in applying this concept of justice in determining the applicable law.

Now we come to the second question: Do juries have a legal right to exercise their power? The courts have had two views on this question, as gleaned from decisions.

At the time of the Revolution, the colonists had strong resentment against the arbitrary exercise of power by the colonial judges, and hence the idea that a jury could find the law was quite popular. This idea found acceptance in some courts. The few decided cases available on the subject come from the federal courts. The first federal decision came in a case involving illegal privateering tried in the United States Supreme Court in Philadelphia in 1793.[1] Justice Wilson charged the jury in a few words "that they, in their general verdict, must decide both the law and the facts." This was a clear and precise pronouncement. The second decision came in a civil case in the United States Supreme Court in 1794,[2] tried by a special jury, brought to determine whether the State of Georgia or the defendant Brailsford had prior rights in a fund sequestered by the State of Georgia during the Revolution, wherein the jury found for the defendant. Chief Justice Jay charged the jury in this way: "It may not be amiss, here, gentlemen, to remind you of the good old rule, that on the questions of fact, it is the province of the jury, on questions of law, it is the province of the court to decide. But it may be observed, that by the same law, which recognizes this reasonable distribution of jurisdiction, you have, nevertheless, a right to take it upon yourselves to judge of both, and to determine the law as well as the facts in controversy. On this, and on every other occasion, however, we have no doubt, you will pay that respect which is due to the opinion of the court; for as on the one hand, it is presumed, that jurors are the better judges of the facts; it is, on the other hand, presumable, that the court [sic] are the best judges of law. But still, both objects are lawfully within your power of decision."

This opinion held good until 1835 when one Battiste was tried for the illegal transportation of slaves into the country. In this case Justice Story wrote: "My opinion is that the jury are no more judges of the law in a capital or other criminal case, upon the plea of not guilty, than they are in every civil case, tried upon the general issue. In each of these cases, their verdict, when general, is compounded of law and of fact and includes both. In each they must necessarily determine the law

[1] U.S. v. Henfield, Wharton's State Trials (U.S.S.C. 1793).
[2] Georgia v. Brailsford, 3 Dahl 1 (U.S.S.C. 1794).

as well as the fact. In each they have the physical power to disregard the law as laid down to them by the Court. But I deny, that in any case, civil or criminal, they have the moral right to decide the law according to their own notions, or pleasure. On the contrary, I hold that the most sacred constitutional right of every party accused of crime, that the jury should respond as to the facts, and the Court as to the law. It is the duty of the Court to instruct the jury as to the law; and it is the duty of the jury to follow the law, as it is handed down by the Court. This is the right of every citizen; and it is his only protection."[3]

None of these cases reviews the historical background, but they do show up a judicial change of viewpoint. The federal courts now act according to the opinion of Justice Story. The same conflict in opinion was shown in the state courts. Here also there are few opinions of record, but two are outstanding studies of the historical grounds for support of contrary viewpoints.

The first of these was in the Supreme Court of Vermont in 1848 involving violation of the liquor license law.[4] The appeal was from a refusal to charge that the jury was judge of both law and fact. The opinion reads in part: "I conclude then, that when political power is conferred on a tribunal without restriction or control, it may be lawfully exerted; that the power of a jury in a criminal case to determine the whole matter at issue committed to their charge, is such a power, and may thereafter be lawfully and rightfully exercised; in short, that such a power is equivalent to, or rather, is itself, a legal right. . . . The extent of jurisdiction of a court or jury is measured by what they may or may not decide with legal effect, and not by the correctness or error of their decisions."

This decision was rejected by the Supreme Court of Maine in 1863,[5] when the court repudiated the idea that a jury is judge of the law. A summary of that opinion is that all people,

[3] U.S. v. Battiste, 2 Summer's Cir. Ct. Reports (1835).
[4] State v. Crouteau, 23 Vt. 14 (1848).
[5] State v. Wright, 53 Me. 328 (1863).

including judges and jurors, have an equal duty to accept and apply law; that the judge knows the law and is the best guide to what is the law, and hence is the source of a jury's knowledge of the law; that if the law of the case is left to the decision of a jury there cannot be consistency in law; and that the power of trial judges and appellate judges to review matters of law involved in jury trials is inconsistent with the right of the jury to be in any sense judges of the law. This view has been consistently followed by the judiciary in America ever since.

It appears then that it took a considerable period of time for the courts to freeze the judicial opinion of jury power. It seems that it will take a longer time to educate the public to accept the judicial view, if indeed it can ever be done, due to the fact that the appellate courts can view trials objectively while jurors act in the field of emotions present in a trial.

If the layman expressed his view, it would be that he accepts the judicial view of jury power in trials in general but uses jury power over law when his sense of justice so requires. He will, in other words, refuse to follow instructions. The public has never been indoctrinated to either view as applicable in all cases. The result is that judges persist in instructing according to the majority legalistic view, and juries persist in acting on the layman's sense-of-justice view.

This situation existed and was known to the framers of the federal and original state constitutions. They considered jury trials and acted specifically in abolishing attaint and in providing that in trials of criminal libel the jury should be the judge of law and fact. Yet the framers did not provide that judges should pass on the law; nor that juries should not pass on the law. They were satisfied in general litigation to leave the majority view and the layman's view counterpoised. It appears that by silence they ratified the counterpoised positions as law and perpetuated them deliberately.

An incidental result of this situation is that juries are ahead of the law at times. Juries, being responsive to shifts in the concept of community justice, will apply some newly developed concept so consistently that litigants must look to the jury concept rather than the law in determining the probable outcome of litigation. As an example, in those states where the established law is that a plaintiff cannot recover any damages if he contributed, even in the slightest way, to the defendant's negligence, juries, in line with the community concept, repeatedly bring in verdicts in favor of plaintiffs who *did* contribute to the negligence; the jurors will only *reduce* the amount of damages if contributory negligence is involved. This shows they will not accept the defense of contributing negligence as a complete bar to recovery, regardless of the established law.

One instance of such action can be stated. A coal truck and a passenger automobile collided in a street intersection. The operator of the passenger automobile sued for the damage to his automobile and personal injuries. The foreman of the jury said after the trial that the jury found both operators to be negligent. In that event, in that jurisdiction, the plaintiff was not entitled to recover and the jury had been so instructed. Asked about this deviation from instruction, the foreman said: "The truck was not damaged and we felt both should share the loss. So we gave the passenger car operator his automobile damage and let him stand for his injuries."

There have been and there will be attempts to make alterations in the jury trial system. As to this, a quotation in an 1853 Ohio case is appropriate. A man was brought to trial on a charge of assault. The legislature had recently provided that in this type of case the jury should consist of six jurors. A jury of six was called. The defendant objected that it was not a legally constituted jury because the Ohio Constitution provided that the right to jury trial shall be inviolate. The conviction was reversed because the constitutional right to jury trial was held to mean a common law trial by twelve jurors. In reference to this proposed change the opinion includes the quotation:

An institution that has so long stood the trying tests of time and experience, that has so long been guarded with scrupulous care, and commanded the admiration of so many of the wise and good, justly demands our jealous scrutiny when innovations are attempted to be made upon it.[6]

This account of the power of juries and the exercise of power by juries is no revelation. All of this has been known for centuries. Yet no substantial change has been demanded or made. This is indicative that the community is satisfied with the placement of such power and the manner in which the power has been exercised. Trial judges have difficulty in swallowing jury verdicts now and then, but they appreciate the responsibility lifted from them by juries. Appellate courts are the least receptive to the exercise of jury power, perhaps because they are furthest from the people.

Those who adversely criticize the jury trial system ignore the fact that constitutional government can hardly function smoothly without the right to jury trial. The fact that a sizable per cent of all trials are held without a jury is evidence of public confidence in the integrity of judges. From time to time, trials are held which arouse the interest and emotion of the public, and the public forms a definite opinion as to what the verdict should be.

If a judge should decide such a case against popular opinion, his act would adversely affect public confidence in the judiciary. If juries decide such cases against the popular opinion, the juries get the blame. As each jury is transient, the blame has no focal point. A verdict contrary to popular opinion receives less condemnation, as each member of the public concludes that, had he been on the jury, he might have reached the same verdict. As confidence in the courts is essential to the maintenance of government, this insulating effect of juries is of inestimable value.

Juries also serve as a whipping boy for losing litigants, their lawyers—and judges. The conduct of the trial is not examined by them to determine what their mistakes were and how these mistakes affected the verdict. Instead, the blame is placed on

[6] Work v. State of Ohio, 2 Ohio State 297 (1853).

the jury. Hence, litigants can salve their wounds by placing the blame on a jury; lawyers can give inadequate service to their clients and salve their pride by placing the blame on a jury; judges can be inefficient in conducting a trial and place the blame on juries.

The American public insists on fair trials, insists on justice in law, and insists that juries have the power to mete out justice. This insistence cannot be quelled in our free society. Juries are the means whereby community justice can be applied, they have the power to apply it, they do apply it, and their act in so doing meets with public approval.

Freedom from restraint allows the exercise of the great power of juries. This power is tempered by the sobering effect of great responsibility. A juror is and feels himself to be an integral part of our system of self-government. Power and responsibility give dignity to jury service and propel jurors to perform this civic duty ably.

The verdict of a jury does not necessarily terminate litigation, except when the verdict is not guilty. In such a case, the defendant cannot again be put in jeopardy (tried again) for the offense charged. In all other cases persistent litigants can, by appeal to higher courts, delay the conclusion of a case for a long period of time, at great expense to themselves and to the public.

17

A New Trial

THE threat of attaint at the common law made jury duty a real hazard, and sitting on an attaint jury became repulsive, so evasion of jury duty became somewhat of a problem. The judges then thought up a way to avoid attaint and put it into effect early in the seventeenth century. The idea was to assume the authority to review a case and grant a new trial. The granting of a new trial wiped out the first trial so the jurors on the first trial could not be charged with attaint and there was no need for an attaint jury. This new idea was applied first in civil cases and later in criminal cases.

The authority to grant a new trial gave the judges what is perhaps their greatest opportunity to determine the outcome of litigation. For, if a jury went contrary to the ideas and will of the judge, he could set aside the verdict and grant a new trial. The setting aside of a verdict and the granting of a new trial usually cannot be questioned on appeal until after the new trial. This strengthens the power of the judge to exercise discretion, good or bad, in granting or denying a new trial. This power to set aside a jury verdict and grant a new trial affords the greatest opportunity for a judge to exercise bias or favoritism. The general rule that the action on this motion is not subject to immediate appeal has exceptions in about four states.

At the present time, a motion for a new trial made by the loser at a civil trial may generally be coupled with a motion for judgment for the loser. If, say, a verdict is for the plaintiff, it may be set aside and a judgment entered for the defendant. As an example: A girl passenger sued the owner and the operator of an automobile for injuries resulting from the driver's alleged negligence. The jury awarded her twenty thousand dollars against both the owner and the driver. The judge set aside the verdict against both, absolved the owner from damages, and granted a new trial to the driver. This same motion for judgment against the jury's verdict can be made by the accused in criminal cases in federal courts and in the courts of a couple of the states.

There is no requirement that this motion be made. One is free to bypass this motion and file an appeal. The grounds stated in support of this motion are substantially the same as the grounds for an appeal. This motion is usually denied. But, by filing the motion, a litigant has at least been courteous to the judge where error on his part is claimed. The litigant then has a chance to get a new trial, on any error the judge may have committed. At the least, the lawyer receives the judge's opinion on the virtue of the lawyer's reasoning.

The grounds on which a new trial may be granted are essentially that to let the verdict stand would be a miscarriage of justice. The party making the motion must specify the particular reasons on which he bases his motion. Some of the grounds: claimed errors of the judge in ruling on objections to items of evidence to which the party objected at the trial; errors in the instruction to the jurors; errors in refusing to give instructions requested by the party; newly discovered evidence which the party could not be expected to have discovered before the trial; admittance of prejudicial evidence; verdict contrary to instruction; verdict not sustained by the evidence; verdict against the clear weight of the evidence; prejudicial comments of opponents; prejudicial unwarranted argument to the jury by the opponent; misconduct of jurors in reading newspapers, talking to strangers, separating from each other, all in violation of orders given by the judge.

One other possible result of this motion should be noted. A civil defendant, after a large jury award, can move for a new trial because the award is so large as to shock the conscience. In this event, the judge can give the plaintiff the choice of remitting part of the judgment or standing a new trial. If the award is shockingly low, a new trial can be granted.

The argument of this motion is addressed to the trial judge only, and the argument should be supported by citing and reading from reported cases which, as precedents, support the argument. But all too often nothing new is presented, and the judge can be greatly bored by a rehash of arguments made at the trial. A judge once expressed the thought of many judges. He remarked of lawyers: "You come in here with no new arguments and no citation of cases to support your argument. Yet, when you get upstairs on appeal you cite plenty of cases. I do not think you treat the trial judge fairly."

Some state courts hold that courts have inherent power to grant a new trial, that the power is judicial and not a subject for legislation. Some hold that a person has no right to a new trial; that it is a privilege granted by the state constitution or by statute. Some states prohibit judges from granting new trials, while others authorize the judge, of his own volition, to order a new trial within a specified number of days. There is agreement among state courts that a judge may not set aside a conviction and grant a new trial without the consent of the accused person.

⇥ 18 ⇤

Appellate Courts

SINCE appellate courts have authority to set aside jury verdicts, they are a part of the jury trial system. From the earliest times, there have been means by which jury trials can be reviewed. As was pointed out, in the early days of jury trials a new trial could be had by demanding a new trial by a jury of twenty-four members. That procedure was changed in England by setting up appellate courts for the special purpose of hearing appeals from the trial courts. We continue that system, and accordingly the loser in the trial court—except the state in a criminal case—has the right to file an appeal in the next higher court. A statement is filed in which the loser sets forth the errors which he claims occurred in the trial court, together with a statement or a transcript of such of the evidence as is necessary to show the error. Then, in support of the loser's contentions, a brief is filed which argues the reasons and cites previous decisions favorable to the loser. The party who files the appeal is now designated as the appellant and the other party is designated as the appellee. The appellee files a similar brief. Later the appellate court hears oral arguments from the lawyers for both parties and reaches a decision based on the concurrence of a majority of the judges. Decisions are printed and bound so that they become available as a guide for the trial courts and for future decisions.

A plaintiff who has won an award in the trial court has a right to file an appeal on the ground that the amount of damages awarded to him is manifestly too low. Such appeals are few in number as the trial judge has authority to grant a new trial on this ground.

State appellate courts have authority to review the evidence when a stated ground for the appeal is that there is no evidence to support the verdict; that the evidence is insufficient to support the verdict; or that the verdict is against the clear preponderance of the evidence. In brief, they can reverse a verdict if it can be said that a reasonable man could not have reached the conclusion reached by the jury. Relatively few appeals are based on these grounds because the trial judge would most probably have disposed of these issues.

The federal courts are restricted because the Seventh Amendment to the Constitution reads: ". . . no fact tried by a jury shall be otherwise examined in any court of the United States than according to the rules of the common law."

It may be said that appellate courts concern themselves mostly with claimed errors of law, such as errors on the part of the judge in erroneously ruling on the admittance or exclusion of evidence, and error in instructing the jury on the law of the case.

If the appeal is successful, the case is sent back (remanded) to the trial court for a new trial. Errors may occur during the new trial so that another appeal may be filed. By use of the right of appeal, litigation may go on for a long time, and the prolonged litigation may be so expensive as to consume the assets of one or both parties. The financial risk involved in litigation, however, does not seem to deter litigants to an observable extent.

In any appeal, the appellant sets forth all the seemingly worthwhile errors which he claims occurred during the trial. The appellate court is not bound to pass upon and write an opinion on each and every one of the errors claimed. It can and it may rest its decision on one claimed error and ignore the others. This is proper because the court is bound only to decide the law of the case; it is not bound to go beyond that and decide points of law not essential to the decision. To do otherwise would decide points of law in a more or less advisory manner and perhaps fetter the court in some subsequent appeal.

It is at this point that the attitude of appellate judges towards

156

jury trials is brought to light. Those judges who are firm believers in the jury system, who place faith in jurors as people of good sense and average intelligence, will credit jurors with considerable resistance to being prejudiced or led into error. They will be slower to find that sufficient prejudice was aroused in the jurors to warrant setting aside a verdict; slower to find that the judge's instruction led a jury astray; and slower to find that the jury did not properly weigh the evidence. The differences in the viewpoints of judges make it possible that an appellate court of one state will find that reversal is justified, while an appellate court of another state would find to the contrary.

It has been made clear that our system of determining the law applicable to a case is to adhere to the rule of following precedent. This rule is designated as the rule of *stare decisis* which, when translated, means to stand by precedent. The rule, when adhered to, gives stability to law, but to adhere to precedent in every case would not be practical.

People tend to be conservative. This makes them more interested in knowing what the law is than in having correctness in law. And, once the people have adjusted themselves to live by the law as established, they would prefer not to have a court abruptly change it. This is especially true of people in trade and commerce who would prefer that changes in the law take place through legislative action, where all parties affected by the change may appear at hearings and testify for or against the proposal. Departure from the rule of precedent may create unanticipated new liabilities which extend back to beyond the limit of time allowed in which to file a suit. On the other hand, legislation cannot affect events of the past because legislatures cannot enact an ex post facto law.

The desire for the stability of law must, however, be weighed against the desire that law meet the needs of justice in the light of present conditions. So, as population, trade, and industry increase, with resulting added complexity of living, the law must live and grow if it is to fulfill its function. To accomplish this aim, the rule of following precedent must yield at times. The courts are obligated to show respect for the rule of *stare decisis* but they are not bound to apply it rigidly, or to follow it blindly. If they did so they would nullify the basic feature of the common law—the capacity to grow and develop—and would soon render the law inadequate to serve the needs of a changing society.

It has always been an established rule that, when a principle of the common law is found to have been wrong, or when it becomes so out-of-date that the reason for it no longer exists, it is legally and morally proper for appellate courts to change it. Errors made in the past are not to be perpetuated, nor justice denied, out of respect for antiquity.

When all of the judges of an appellate court agree to depart from the rule of precedent and thus make a change from prior law, their action meets with little, if any, criticism by the public. But when the judges disagree, the public can be expected to wonder if the change was wise. When the minority judges not only fail to agree to change but are upset to the extent that they write opinions criticizing the majority, the public loses a bit of its confidence in the wisdom of the majority judges. Two instances will illustrate both the departure from the rule of precedent and the judicial criticism provoked thereby.

One instance of judicial protest came in a case involving the changing of the legal view of insanity to a more scientific basis. The appeal was taken by a man convicted of manslaughter, who had raised the issue of insanity. Over a period of four years he had been examined at various times by eleven psychiatrists who either were government employees or had been appointed by the court. At the trial two policemen testified that after being arrested and while in their custody the accused had acted sane. Five or six of the psychiatrists testified that they could not diagnose the defendant's condition on the morning of the killing due to the lapse of time between the crime and their examinations. Five, from similar data, testified that the defendant was insane at the time of the crime, and one testified that the act was the product of mental infirmity. The jury found the accused to have been sane and convicted him. On appeal, six of the nine judges making up the appellate court reversed the conviction, holding that reasonable jurymen could not conclude beyond a reasonable doubt that the defendant was sane at the time of the shooting.[1]

This conclusion was vigorously protested by the three minority judges as an invasion of the jury function and as a serious departure from the rule of precedent that jurors had exclusive power to pass on credibility of witnesses and the weight of the evidence. The minority opinion contains these statements: "The evidence therefore presented a typical jury question which conceivably could have been decided either way. The decision was for the jury however, and not for us; we have no right whatever to substitute our judgment for that of the jury where there is evidence to support its verdict, no matter what evidence there may have been to the contrary and no matter how much we may wish to decide the question the other way. . . . Traditionally such a finding cannot be disturbed on appeal. I suggest that stable rules of law and consistent application of them are essential to the guidance of bench and bar in trial practice and procedure."

This protest was not without effect. Two years later the court retracted in another case[2] with this statement: "We emphasize that, since the question of whether the defendant had a disease or defect is ultimately for the triers of the fact, obviously its resolution cannot be controlled by expert opinion. The jury must determine for itself, from all the testimony, lay and expert, whether the nature and degree of the disability are sufficient to establish a mental disease or defect as we have defined these terms." The opinion also included this statement: "What psychiatrists may consider a mental disease or defect for clinical purposes, where their concern is treatment, may or may not be the same as mental disease or defect for the jury's purpose in determining criminal responsibility."

The other instance is that in 1944 the United States Supreme Court had before it a case in which a seaman sued to recover

[1] U.S. v. Wright, 250 F2 24 (1957).
[2] U.S. v. McDonald (1962) 312 F2 847 (1962).

damages for injuries received while at sea by a fall from a staging, which gave way when a piece of defective rope, holding it up, parted.[3] The bad rope had been supplied by a mate from a supply room where there was ample sound rope available for use. The question was whether the defect in the staging due to the defective rope was a breach of the warranty of seaworthiness thus rendering the owner of the ship liable. The trial judge relied on a United States Supreme Court decision rendered in 1928 involving a seaman injured under almost identical conditions.[4] That opinion contained the statement: "The record does not support the suggestion that the Pinar Del Rio was unseaworthy. The mate selected a bad rope when good ones were available." The seaman lost the case. The trial judge followed the rule of precedent so established and held that any right the seaman had was under the British Workman's Compensation Act and accordingly recovery of damages was denied in the trial court.

The case was carried to the Circuit Court of Appeals which sustained, but on the ground that no lien existed against the ship. An appeal to the United States Supreme Court followed. The Supreme Court departed from the rule of precedent, and reversed its previous decision saying: "So far as this statement [quoted in the preceding paragraph] supports these assumptions [of the judges below], it is disproved." The case was remanded for a new trial.

Justice Roberts wrote a minority opinion in this case in which Justice Frankfurter concurred as follows: "The tendency to disregard precedents in the decision of cases like the present has become so strong in this court of late as, in my view to shake confidence in the consistency of decisions and leave the courts below on an uncharted sea of doubt and difficulty without any confidence that what was said yesterday will be held good tomorrow, unless indeed a modern instance grows into a custom of members of this court to make public announcement of a change of views and to indicate that they will change

[3] Plamals v. The Pinar Del Rio, 277 U.S. 151 (1928).
[4] Mahnick v. Southern Steamship Co., 321 U.S. 96 (1944).

160

their votes on the same question when another case comes before the court. This might, to some extent, obviate the predicament in which the lower courts, the bar, and the public find themselves."

Such criticisms, as in the two instances noted, are known to the members of the court who participated in the majority opinion, as they see the draft of them before the decisions are printed. These decisions were handed down by the majority in spite of the accompanying criticisms.

The two cases used as illustrations are not intended to question the correctness of the decisions or the authority to make them. They are given solely to illustrate the points that top court decisions do change the law by departing from the rule of precedent, that departure is sometimes criticized by the minority members of the court, and to illustrate that there is always a tentative quality to law.

Departure from the rule of precedent is unusual, but it does occur. The fact that it does occur is a reason for many appeals based on the possibility and hope that the appellate court will, in a particular case, depart from the rule.

The top court, having the final determination, determines the law for the state with finality. As that court determines only those principles which are submitted, there may be in each state several or many principles of common law on which the top court has not ruled. This leaves the trial judge to find the correct principle and to apply the principle correctly. This he does by a search of his top court decisions to find out if that court has ruled on the principle. If it has not ruled on the principle, he next compares the legal problem with comparable problems that have been decided. Then he examines if and how top courts of other states have decided the principle. All the while, he is attempting to forecast what his top court would decide if the question should reach it.

This explanation of the authority of appellate courts to depart from the rule of precedent makes clear that the instructions on the law given by the trial judge to the jury have tentative applicability. There are many instances in which he must give instructions when he has no certainty that his instruction will be held to be correct. The tentative basis on which a trial judge acts, and the manner in which appellate courts act, is well illustrated in a case which was decided by the top court of the District of Columbia in 1942.[5]

A private nurse was attending a patient in a hospital owned and operated by a charitable corporation. She was injured through the negligence of a student nurse of the hospital and filed a suit against the hospital corporation for damages. The filing of the suit presented to the court the question whether the charitable corporation was liable for damages to persons injured through the negligence of its employees. The hospital asserted that it had, by the common law, immunity from suit. The judge was obligated to make a decision without delay. If he found that the hospital had immunity he would direct a verdict for the hospital. At this time, there was no applicable decision in the top court. In fact, that court in 1938 had declined to decide the point, as the case before it could be disposed of on other issues. Three previous suits filed in the trial court had been dismissed on the basis of immunity.

The history of charitable corporation immunity showed to the judge that it had arisen in England in 1839 on this basis: "To give damages out of a trust fund would not be to apply it to those objects whom the author of the fund had in view, but would divert it to a completely different purpose." This concept was followed in other English cases in 1846 and 1861. Massachusetts and Maryland adopted that concept in 1876 and 1885, respectively. The concept was later accepted in several states, but courts in some states would not rule for full immunity to charitable corporations, allowing or denying it on such factors as whether the person who suffered the damage was a paying patient or a non-paying patient; the nature of the negligence; whether damage occurred in or outside the hospital; whether the person was identified with the hospital or was a stranger to it; and the nature of the employment of the negligent employee.

[5] Hughes v. Pres. Georgetown College, 130 F2 810 (1942).

The trial judge chose to hold that liability existed on the ground that the plaintiff was a stranger to the hospital. After a verdict for the plaintiff, the hospital appealed.

The appellate court looked into the law on immunity. It found that the English cases on which the trial judge had relied had been reversed in England in 1866 and 1871. This fact was seemingly not known to the courts of Massachusetts and Maryland, so that those courts had in fact adopted the *opposite* of the existing English common law. The appellate court also found that there no longer existed grounds to claim that the assets of the charity might be depleted, because the hospital could purchase liability insurance at reasonable cost. On these two grounds, the court ruled that the hospital corporation had no immunity whatever but was subject to suit, the same as any individual. The top court acted for sound and legal reasons because it found that American courts had applied neither the correct English law nor the correct precedent, and because the basis for immunity no longer existed, due to the availability of liability insurance.

A juror has little, if any, realization of how much thought, study, time, and money have been expended to bring about the determination of the principles of law which are applied during a trial. Nor does he realize how much thought and study have gone into determining the correct principles of law contained in the judge's charge to the jury. It is interesting to speculate whether individualistic and perverse jurors would be less inclined to use the jury power, to go contrary to the judge's instructions, if they knew and realized that his instructions could not have been given if prior litigants and judges had not gone to the great expense and study which made the instructions possible.

Each of the original states had begun its existence with the same common law, and each state had reserved the right to determine what part of the common law it would retain as applicable to its situation; how it would allow the common law to develop to meet changed conditions, and how it would interpret its statutes. No state is obligated to accept the construction placed on law by another state. This means that appellate courts of each state shape the law applicable in that state. As a consequence, we can and do have divergence of law from state to state, so that an act found to be wrong in one state is not necessarily found to be a wrong in another state.

EPILOGUE

"How Scrupulously Delicate"

On the first page of this book it was stated that the word "law" defies definition. Now we are able to define at least a part of law as being a determination of, or pronouncement of, rights and obligations after a trial. If the trial is by a jury, the law of the particular case is determined by the jury, and pronouncement of the law is made by the jury verdict. The verdict makes the law of the case, unless it is set aside and a new trial ordered. The final jury verdict is the law of the case.

Another case may come to trial which, at the outset, apparently is parallel to the first case. It may terminate in an opposite verdict merely because a different weight was given to items of evidence.

The result is that in considering law in its application to everyday activity, we are obliged to act on the principles of law, but we must act tentatively. Whether our acts are lawful, whether we can successfully enforce our ideas of rights and duties, will not be determined until the facts are submitted under court procedure and a final finding or verdict is determined. Not until then can we definitely know our rights and duties. This situation explains why able lawyers cannot advise laymen of the law in its application to instances where there exists any uncertainty as to the facts or the applicable law.

In spite of the unpredictability of verdicts, we are fortunate in having a jury trial system as a part of a free society which seeks to preserve rule by law rather than rule by men. No better system has yet been devised to determine facts. Whatever faults it may have have proven to be endurable. It is embedded in our society as practical, necessary, and acceptable. Few persons would care to predict that our society would long remain peaceable if the right to a jury trial did not exist.

Our society must maintain an equitable balance between the rights and immunities of individuals and the rights of the community as a whole. As our population grows, new public necessities arise which are in conflict with the rights of individuals. In the solution of this conflict, the trend is to expand the field of public rights and to diminish the field of individual rights. Witness the imposition of a tax on individual income. This trend cannot be stopped so long as we expand our population.

The jury system is not above criticism. One criticism is that juries are drawn from the middle class in our society and therefore are not truly representative. Another criticism is that jury trials are too time-consuming. This is a valid criticism, but the critics, failing to place responsibility for the consumption of time, let one assume that it is due to the system. However, an observer of several jury trials will place responsibility for consumption of time more on the lawyers than on the system.

It is fitting to close with the comment made by the immortal Blackstone: "We may here again observe, and observing we cannot but admire, how scrupulously delicate and how impartially just the law of England [substitute the United States] approves itself, in the constitution and frame of a tribunal, thus excellently contrived for the test and investigation of truth; which appears most remarkably: 1. In the avoiding of frauds and secret management, by electing the twelve jurors out of the whole panel by lot. 2. In its caution against all impartiality and bias, by guarding the whole panel or array, if the officer returning is suspected to be other than indifferent; and repelling particular jurors, if probable cause be shown of malice or favor to either party."

Appendices

APPENDIX A

Blackstone's
"The Nature of Laws in General"[1]

LAW, in its most general and comprehensive sense, signifies a rule of action, and is applied indiscriminately to all kinds of action, whether animate or inanimate, rational or irrational. Thus we say, the laws of motion, of gravitation, of optics, or mechanics, as well as the laws of nature and of nations. And it is that rule of action which is prescribed by some superior and which the inferior is bound to obey.

Thus when the Supreme Being formed the universe, and created matter out of nothing, He impressed certain principles upon that matter, from which it can never depart, and without which it would cease to be. When He put the matter into motion, He established certain laws of motion, to which all movable bodies must conform. And to descend from the greatest operations to the smallest, when a workman forms a clock, or other piece of mechanism, he establishes at his own pleasure certain arbitrary laws for its direction; as that the hand shall describe a given space in a given time; to which law as long as the work conforms, so long it continues in perfection, and answers the end of its formation.

If we further advance, from mere inactive matter to vegetable and animal life, we shall find them still governed by laws; more numerous, indeed, but equally fixed and invariable. The whole progress of plants, from the seed to the root, and from thence to the seed again; the method of animal nutrition, digestion, secretion and all other branches of vital economy, are not left to chance, or the will of the creature itself, but are per-

---

[1] Harper Brothers. 21st London Edition, 1854. The first lecture, seven immaterial paragraphs of which are omitted.

formed in a wondrous involuntary manner, and guided by unerring rules laid down by the great Creator.

This, then, is the general signification of law, a rule of action dictated by some superior being: and, in those creatures that have neither the power to think, nor the will, such laws must be invariably obeyed, so long as the creature itself subsists, for its existence depends on that obedience. But laws, in their more confined sense, and in which it is our present business to consider them, denote the rules, not of action in general, but of human action or conduct: that is, the precepts by which man, the noblest of all sublunary beings, a creature endowed with both reason and free will, is commanded to make use of these facilities in the general regulation of his behavior.

Man, considered as a creature, must necessarily be subject to the laws of his Creator, for he is entirely a dependent being. A being, independent of any other, has no rule to pursue, but such as he prescribes to himself; but a state of dependence will inevitably oblige the inferior to take the will of him on whom he depends as the rule of his conduct; not indeed in every particular, but in all those points wherein his dependence consists. This principle, therefore, has more or less intent and effect, in proportion as the superiority of the one and the dependence of the other is greater or less, absolute or limited.

This will of his Maker is called the law of nature. For as God, when He created matter, and endued it with a principle of mobility, established certain rules for the perpetual direction of that motion; so, when He created man, and endued him with free-will to conduct himself in all parts of life, He laid down certain immutable laws of human nature, whereby that free-will is in some degree regulated and restrained, and gave him also the faculty of reason to discover the purport of those laws.

Considering the Creator only as a Being of infinite power, He was able, unquestionably, to have prescribed whatever laws He pleased to His creature, man, however unjust or severe. But as He is also a Being of infinite wisdom, He has laid down only such laws as were founded in those relations of jus-

170

tice, that existed in the nature of things antecedent to any positive precept. These are the eternal, immutable laws of good and evil, to which the Creator Himself in all His dispensations conforms: and which He has enabled human reason to discover, so far as they are necessary for the conduct of human actions. Such, among others, are these principles: that we should live honestly, should hurt nobody, and should render to everyone his due; to which three general precepts Justinian has reduced the whole doctrine of law.

But if the discovery of these first principles of the law of nature depended only upon the due exertion of right reason, and could not otherwise be obtained than by a chain of metaphysical disquisitions, mankind would have wanted some inducement to have quickened their inquiries, and the greater part of the world would have rested content in mental indolence, and ignorance its inseparable companion. As, therefore, the Creator is a Being, not only of infinite power, and wisdom, but also of infinite goodness, He has been pleased so to contrive the constitution and frame of humanity, that we should want no other prompter to inquire after and pursue the rule of right, but only our own self-love, that universal principle of action, for He has so intimately connected, so inseparably interwoven the laws of eternal justice with the happiness of each individual, that the latter cannot be attained but by observing the former; and, if the former be punctually obeyed, it cannot but induce the latter. In consequence of which mutual connection of justice and human felicity, He has not perplexed the law of nature with a multitude of abstracted rules and precepts, referring merely to the fitness or unfitness of things, as some have vainly surmised; but has graciously reduced the rule of obedience to this one paternal precept, "that man should pursue his own true and substantial happiness." This is the foundation of what we call ethics, or natural law. For the several articles into which it is branched in our systems amount to no more than demonstrating that this or that action tends to man's real happiness, and therefore very justly concluding that the performance of it is a part of the law of nature; or, on the other hand, that this or that action is destructive of man's real happiness, and therefore that the law of nature forbids it.

This law of nature being coeval with mankind, and dictated by God himself, is of course superior in obligation to any other. It is binding over all the globe, in all countries, and at all times; no human laws are of any validity if contrary to this; and such of them as are valid derive all their force and all their authority, mediately or immediately, from this original.

But in order to apply this to the particular exigencies of each individual, it is still necessary to have recourse to reason; whose office it is to discover, as was before observed, what the law of nature directs in every circumstance of life; by considering what method will tend the most effectually to our own substantial happiness. And if our reason were always, as in our first ancestor before his transgression, clear and perfect, unimpaired by disease or intemperance, the task would be pleasant and easy; we should need no other guide than this. But every man now finds the contrary in his own experience; that his reason is corrupt, and his understanding full of ignorance and error.

If man were to live in a state of nature, unconnected with other individuals, there would be no occasion for any other laws than the law of nature and the law of God. Neither could any other law possibly exist: for a law always supposes some superior who is to make it; and in a state of nature we are all equal, without any other superior but Him who is the author of our being. But man was formed for society; and, as is demonstrated by the writers on this subject, is neither capable of living alone, nor, indeed has the courage to do it. However, as it is impossible for the whole race of mankind to be united in one great society, they must necessarily divide into many, and form separate states, commonwealths, and nations, entirely independent of each other, and yet liable to a mutual intercourse. Hence arises a third kind of law to regulate this mutual intercourse called "the law of nations"; which, as none of these states will acknowledge a superiority in the other, cannot be dictated by any, but depends entirely upon the rules of natural law, or upon mutual compacts, treaties, leagues, and agreements between these several communities; in the construction, also, of which compacts we have no other rule to resort to but the law of nature; being the only one to which all communities are equally subject, and therefore the civil law very justly observes (that that rule which natural reason has dictated to all men, is called the law of nations).

Thus much I thought it necessary to premise concerning the law of nature, and the law of nations, before I proceeded to treat more fully of the principal subject of this section, municipal or civil law; that is, the rule by which particular districts, communities, or nations are governed. I call it municipal law, in compliance with common speech; for, though strictly that expression denotes the particular customs of one single municipium or free town, yet it may with sufficient propriety be applied to any one state or nation, which is governed by the same laws and customs.

Municipal law, thus understood, is properly defined to be "a rule of civil conduct prescribed by the supreme power in a state, commanding what is right, and prohibiting what is wrong." Let us endeavor to explain its several properties, as they arise out of this definition.

And, first, it is a rule, not a transient sudden order from a superior to or concerning a particular person; but something permanent, uniform, and universal. Therefore, a particular act of legislature to confiscate the goods of Titius, or to attaint him of high treason, does not enter into the idea of a municipal law, for the operation of this act is spent upon Titius only, and has no relation to the community in general; it is rather a sentence than a law. But an act to declare that the crime of which Titius is accused shall be deemed high treason; this has permanency, uniformity, and universality, and therefore is properly a rule. It also is called a rule to distinguish it from advice or counsel, which we are at liberty to follow or not, as we see proper, and to judge upon the reasonableness or unreasonableness of the thing advised; whereas our obedience to the law depends not upon our approbation, but upon the Maker's will.

173

Counsel is only matter of persuasion, law is matter of injunction; counsel acts only upon the willing, law upon the unwilling also.

It is also called a rule, to distinguish it from a compact or agreement; for a compact is a promise proceeding from us, law is a command directed to us. The language of a compact is, "I will, or will not, do this"; that of a law is, "thou shalt, or shalt not, do it." It is true there is an obligation which a compact carries with it, equal in point of conscience to that of a law; but then the original of the obligation is different. In compacts, we ourselves determine and promise what shall be done before we are obliged to do it; in laws, we are obliged to act without ourselves determining or promising anything at all. Upon these accounts law is defined to be "a rule."

Municipal law is also "a rule of civil conduct." This distinguishes municipal law from the natural or revealed; the former of which is the rule of moral conduct, and the latter not only the rule of moral conduct, but also the rule of faith. These regard man as a creature, and point out his duty to God, to himself, and to his neighbor, considered in the light of an individual. But municipal or civil law regards him also as a citizen, and bound to other duties towards his neighbor than those of mere nature and religion; duties which he has engaged in by enjoying the benefits of the common union; and which amount to no more than that he do contribute, on his part, to the subsistence and peace of the society.

It is likewise "a rule prescribed." Because a bare resolution, confined in the breast of the legislator, without manifesting itself by some external sign, can never be properly a law. It is requisite that this resolution be notified to the people who are to obey it. But the manner in which this notification is to be made, is matter of very great indifference. It may be notified by universal tradition and long practice, which supposes a previous publication, and is the case of the common law of England. It may be notified, viva voce (orally), by officers appointed for that purpose, as is done with regard to proclamations, and such acts of parliament as are appointed, to be publicly read in

174

churches and other assemblies. It may, lastly, be notified by writing, printing, or the like, which is the general course taken with all our acts of parliament. Yet, whatever way is made use of, it is incumbent on the promulgators to do it in the most public and perspicuous manner. There is still a more unreasonable method than this, which is called making of laws ex post facto (which relate back in time), when after an action (indifferent in itself) is committed, the legislature then for the first time declares it to have been a crime, and inflicts a punishment upon the person who has committed it. Here it is impossible that the party could foresee that an action, innocent when it was done, should be afterwards converted to guilt by a subsequent law; he had, therefore, no cause to abstain from it; and all punishment for not abstaining must of consequence be cruel and unjust. All laws should be, therefore, made to commence in futuro (future), and be notified before their commencement; which is implied in the term "prescribed." But when this rule is in the usual manner notified or prescribed, it is then the subject's business to be thoroughly acquainted therewith; for if ignorance of what he might know, were admitted as a legitimate excuse, the laws would be of no effect, but might always be eluded with impunity.

But further: municipal law is "a rule of civil conduct prescribed by the supreme power in a state." For legislature, as was before observed, is the greatest act of superiority that can be exercised by one being over another. Wherefore it is requisite to the very essence of a law, that it be made by the supreme power. Sovereignty and legislature are indeed convertible terms; one cannot subsist without the other.

This may lead us into a short inquiry concerning the nature of society and civil government; and the natural, inherent right that belongs to the sovereignty of a state, wherever that sovereignty be lodged, of making and enforcing laws.

The only true and natural foundations of society are the wants and the fears of individuals. Not that we can believe, with some theoretical writers, that there ever was a time when there was no such thing as society either natural or civil; but that, from the impulse of reason, and through a sense of their wants and weaknesses, individuals met together in a large plain, entered into an original contract, and chose the tallest man present to be their governor. This notion, of an actually existing unconnected state of nature, is too wild to be seriously admitted: and besides it is plainly contradictory to the revealed accounts of the primitive origin of mankind, and their preservation two thousand years afterwards; both which were effected by the means of single families. These formed the first natural society, among themselves; which, every day extending its limits, laid the first though imperfect rudiments of civil or political society: and when it grew too large to subsist with convenience in that pastoral state, wherein the patriarchs appear to have lived, it necessarily subdivided itself by various migrations into more. Afterwards, as agriculture increased, which employs and can maintain a much greater number of hands, migrations became less frequent: and various tribes, which had formerly separated, reunited again; sometimes by compulsion and conquest, sometimes by accident, and sometimes, perhaps, by compact. But though society had not its formal beginning from any convention of individuals, actuated by their wants and their fears; yet it is the sense of their weakness and imperfection that keeps mankind together, that demonstrates the necessity of this union, and that, therefore, is the solid and natural foundation, as well as the cement, of civil society. And this is what we mean by the original contract of society; which, though perhaps in no instance it has ever been formally expressed at the first institution of a state, yet in nature and reason must always be understood and implied, in the very act of associating together; namely, that the whole should protect all its parts, and that every part should pay obedience to the will of the whole; or, in other words, that the community should guard the rights of each individual member, and that (in return for this protection) each individual should submit to the laws of the community; without which submission of all it was impossible that protection could be certainly extended to any.

For when civil society is once formed, government at the

same time, results of course, as necessary to preserve and to keep that society in order. Unless some superior be constituted, whose commands and decisions all the members are bound to obey, they would still remain as in a state of nature, without any judge upon earth to define their several rights, and redress their several wrongs. But, as all the members which compose this society were naturally equal, it may be asked, in whose hands are the reins of government to be entrusted? To this the general answer is easy; but the application of it to particular cases has occasioned one-half of those mischiefs, which are apt to proceed from misguided political zeal. In general, all mankind will agree that government should be reposed in such persons, in whom those qualities are most likely to be found, the perfection of which is among the attributes of Him who is emphatically styled the Supreme Being; the three grand requisites, I mean, of wisdom, of goodness, and of power: wisdom to discern the real interest of the community; goodness, to endeavor always to pursue that real interest; and strength, or power, to carry this knowledge and intention into action. There are the natural foundations of sovereignty, and these are the requisites that ought to be found in every well-constituted frame of government.

How the several forms of government we now see in the world at first actually began is matter of great uncertainty, and has occasioned infinite disputes. However they began, or by what right soever they subsist, there is and must be in all of them a supreme, irresistible, absolute, uncontrolled authority in which the rights of sovereignty reside. And this authority is placed in those hands wherein (according to the opinion of the founders of such respective states, either expressly given, or collected from their tacit approbation) the qualities requisite for supremacy, wisdom, goodness, and power, are the most likely to be found.

In a democracy, where the right of making laws resides in the people at large, public virtue, or goodness of intention, is more likely to be found, than either of the other qualities of government. Popular assemblies are frequently foolish in their contrivance and weak in their execution, but generally mean to do the thing that is right and just, and have always a degree of patriotism or public spirit. In aristocracies there is more wisdom to be found than in the other frames of government, being composed, or intended to be composed, of the most experienced citizens; but there is less honesty than in a republic, and less strength than in a monarchy. A monarchy is, indeed, the most powerful of any; for, by the entire conjunction of the legislative and executive powers, all the sinews of government are knit together and united in the hand of the prince; but then there is imminent danger of his employing that strength to improvident or oppressive purposes.

Thus these three species of government have, all of them, their several perfections and imperfections. Democracies are usually the best calculated to direct the end of the law; aristocracies to invent the means by which that end shall be obtained; and monarchies to carry those means into execution. The ancients, as was observed, had in general no idea of any other permanent form of government but these three: for though Cicero declares himself of opinion, "that the best constituted republic, is that which is duly compounded of these three forms, the monarchical, aristocratic, and democratic"; yet Tacitus treats this notion of a mixed government, formed out of them all, and partaking of the advantages of each, as a visionary whim, and one that, if effected, could never be lasting or secure.

But, happily for us of this island, the British constitution has long remained, and I trust will long continue, a standing exception to the truth of this observation. For, as with us the executive power of the laws is lodged in a single person, they have all the advantages of strength and dispatch that are to be found in the most absolute monarchy: and as the legislature of the kingdom is entrusted to three distinct powers, entirely independent of each other: first, the king; secondly, the lords, spiritual and temporal, which is an aristocratical assembly of persons selected for their piety, their birth, their wisdom, their valor, or their property; and, thirdly, the house of commons, freely chosen by the people from among themselves, which makes it a kind of democracry; as this aggregate body, actuated by different springs, and attentive to different interests, composes the British parliament, and has the supreme disposal of everything, there can be no inconvenience attempted by either of the three branches, but will be withstood by one of the other two; each branch being armed with a negative power sufficient to repel any innovation which it shall think inexpedient or dangerous.

Having thus cursorily considered the three usual species of government, and our own singular constitution, selected and compounded from them all, I proceed to observe, that, as the power of making laws constitutes the supreme authority, so wherever the supreme authority in any state resides, it is the right of that authority to make laws; that is, in the words of our definition, to prescribe the rule of civil action. This may be discovered from the very end and institution of civil states. For a state is a collective body, composed of a multitude of individuals, united for their safety and convenience, and intending to act together as one man. If it, therefore, is to act as one man, it ought to act by one uniform will. But, inasmuch as political communities are made up of many natural persons, each of whom has his particular will and inclination, these several wills cannot by any natural union be joined together, or tempered and disposed into a lasting harmony, so as to constitute and produce that one uniform will of the whole. It can therefore be no otherwise produced than by a political union; by the consent of all persons to submit their own private wills to the will of one man, or of one or more assemblies of men, to whom the supreme authority is entrusted; and this will of that one man, or assemblage of men, is in different states, according to their different constitutions, understood to be law.

Thus far as to the right of the supreme power to make laws; but further, it is its duty likewise. For since the respective members are bound to conform themselves to the will of the state, it is expedient that they receive directions from the state declaratory of that its will. But as it is impossible, in so great a multitude, to give injunctions to every particular man, relative to each particular action, it is therefore incumbent on the state to establish general rules, for the perpetual information and direction of all persons in all points, whether of positive or negative duty. And this, in order that every man may know what to look upon as his own, what as another's; what absolute and what relative duties are required at his hands; what is to be esteemed honest, dishonest, or indifferent; what degree every man retains of his natural liberty; what he has given up as the price of the benefits of society; and after what manner each person is to moderate the use and exercise of those rights which the state assigns him, in order to promote and secure the public tranquillity. From what has been advanced, the truth of the former branch of our definition, is (I trust) sufficiently evident; that "municipal law is a rule of civil conduct prescribed by the supreme power in a state." I proceed now to the latter branch of it; that it is a rule so prescribed, "Commanding what is right, and prohibiting what is wrong."

Now, in order to do this completely, it is first of all necessary that the boundaries of right and wrong be established and ascertained by law. And when this is once done, it will follow, of course, that it is likewise the business of the law, considered as a rule of civil conduct, to enforce these rights, and to restrain or redress these wrongs. It remains, therefore, only to consider in what manner the law is said to ascertain the boundaries of right and wrong; and the methods which it takes to command the one and prohibit the other.

For this purpose every law may be said to consist of several parts: one, declaratory; whereby the rights to be observed, and wrongs to be eschewed, are clearly defined and laid down: another, directory; whereby the subject is instructed and enjoined to observe those rights, and to abstain from the commission of those wrongs: a third, remedial; whereby a method is pointed out to recover a man's private rights, or redress his private wrongs: to which may be added a fourth, usually termed the sanction, or vindicatory branch of the law; whereby it is signified what evil or penalty shall be incurred by such as commit any public wrongs, and transgress or neglect their duty.

With regard to the first of these, the declaratory part of the municipal law, this depends not so much upon the law of revelation or of nature as upon the wisdom and will of the legislator. This doctrine, which before was slightly touched, deserves a more particular explication. Those rights, then, which God and nature have established, are therefore called natural rights, such as are life and liberty, need not the aid of human laws to be more effectually invested in everyman than they are; neither do they receive any additional strength when declared by the municipal laws to be inviolable. On the contrary, no human legislature has power to abridge or destroy them, unless the owner shall himself commit some act that amounts to a forfeiture. Neither do divine or natural duties (such as, for instance, the worship of God, the maintenance of children, and the like) receive any stronger sanction from being also declared to be duties by the law of the land. The case is the same as to crimes and misdemeanors, that are forbidden by the superior laws, and therefore styled mala in se (crimes in themselves), such as murder, theft, and perjury; which contract no additional turpitude from being declared unlawful by the inferior legislature. For that legislature in all these cases acts only, as was before observed, in subordination to the great lawgiver, transcribing and publishing His precepts. So that, upon the whole, the declaratory part of the municipal law has no force or operation at all with regard to actions that are naturally and intrinsically right or wrong.

But, with regard to things in themselves indifferent, the case is entirely altered. These become either right or wrong, just or unjust, duties or misdemeanors, according as the municipal legislator sees proper, for promoting the welfare of the society, and more effectually carrying on the purposes of civil life. Thus our own common law has declared that the goods of the wife do instantly, upon marriage, become the property and right of the husband; and our statute law has declared all monopolies a public offense; yet that right and this offense have no foundation in nature, but are merely created by the law for the purposes of civil society. Sometimes, where the thing itself has its rise

181

from the law of nature, the particular circumstances and mode of doing it becomes right or wrong, as the laws of the land shall direct. Thus, for instance, in civil duties, obedience to superiors is the doctrine of revealed as well as natural religion; but who those superiors shall be, and in what circumstances, or to what degrees they shall be obeyed, it is the province of human laws to determine. And so as to injuries or crimes, it must be left to our own legislature to decide in what cases the seizing another's cattle shall amount to a trespass or a theft; and where it shall be a justifiable action, as when a landlord takes them by way of distress for rent.

Thus much for the declaratory part of the municipal law: and the directory stands much upon the same footing; for this virtually includes the former, the declaration being usually collected from the direction. The law that says "thou shalt not steal" implies a declaration that stealing is a crime. And we have seen that, in things naturally indifferent, the very essence of right and wrong depends upon the direction of the laws to do or to omit them.

The remedial part of a law is so necessary a consequence of the former two, that laws must be very vague and imperfect without it, for in vain would rights be declared, in vain directed to be observed, if there were no method of recovering and asserting those rights, when wrongfully withheld or invaded. This is what we mean, properly, when we speak of the protection of the law. When, for instance, the declaratory part of the law has said "that the field or inheritance, which belonged to Titius' father, is vested by his death in Titius"; and the directory part has "forbidden anyone to enter on another's property, without the leave of the owner"; if Gaius, after this will presume to take possession of the land, the remedial part of the law will then interpose its office: will make Gaius restore the possession to Titius, and also pay him damages for the invasion.

With regard to the sanction of laws, or the evil that may attend the breach of public duties, it is observed that human legislators have for the most part chosen to make the sanction of their laws rather vindicatory than remuneratory, or to consist rather in punishments than in actual particular rewards. Because, in the first place, the quiet enjoyment and protection of all our civil rights and liberties, which are the sure and general consequence of obedience to the municipal law, are in themselves the best and most valuable of all rewards. Because also, were the exercise of every virtue to be enforced by the proposal of particular rewards, it were impossible for any state to furnish stock enough for so profuse a bounty. And further, because the dread of evil is a much more forcible principle of human actions than the prospect of good. For which reasons, though a prudent bestowing of rewards is sometimes of exquisite use, yet we find that those civil laws, which enforce and enjoin our duty, do seldom, if ever, propose any privilege or gift to such as obey the law; but do constantly come armed with a penalty denounced against transgressors, either expressly defining the nature and quantity of the punishment, or else leaving it to the discretion of the judges, and those who are entrusted with the care of putting the laws in execution.

Of all the parts of a law the most effectual is the vindicatory; for it is but lost labor to say, "do this, or avoid that," unless we also declare "this shall be the consequence of your noncompliance." We must therefore observe, that the main strength and force of a law consists in the penalty annexed to it. Herein is to be found the principal obligation of human laws.

Legislators and their laws are said to compel and oblige: not that by any natural violence they so constrain a man as to render it impossible for him to act otherwise than as they direct, which is the strict sense of obligation; but because, by declaring and exhibiting a penalty against offenders, they bring it to pass that no man can easily choose to transgress the law; since by reason of the impending correction, compliance is in a high degree preferable to disobedience. And even where rewards are proposed as well as punishments threatened, the obligation of the law seems chiefly to consist in the penalty; for rewards, in their nature can only persuade and allure; nothing is compulsory but punishment.

It is true, it hath been holden, and very justly, by the principal of our ethical writers, that human laws are binding upon men's consciences; but if that were the only or most forcible obligation, the good only would regard the laws, and the bad would set them at defiance. And, true as this principle is, it must still be understood with some restriction. It holds, I apprehend, as to rights; and that, when the law has determined the field to belong to Titius, it is matter of conscience no longer to withhold or to invade it. So also in regard to natural duties and such offenses as are mala in se: here we are bound in conscience, because we are bound by superior laws, before those human laws were in being, to perform the one and abstain from the other. But in ... ...tion to those laws which enjoin only positive duties, and forbid only such things as are not mala in se but mala prohibita merely, without any intermixture of moral guilt, annexing a penalty to noncompliance, here I apprehend conscience is no further concerned than by directing a submission to the penalty, in case of our breach of those laws, for otherwise the multitude of penal laws in a state would not only be looked upon as an impolitic, but would also be a very wicked thing, if every such law were a snare for the conscience of the subject. But in these cases the alternative is offered to every man, "either abstain from this, or submit to such a penalty"; and his conscience will be clear, whichever side of the alternative he thinks proper to embrace. Thus, by the statutes for preserving the game, a penalty is denounced against every unqualified person that kills a hare, and against every person who possesses a partridge in August. And so, too, by other statutes, pecuniary penalties are inflicted for exercising trades without serving an apprenticeship thereto, for not burying the dead in woolen, for not performing the statute work on the public roads, and for innumerable other positive misdemeanors. Now these prohibitory laws do not make the transgression a moral offense, or sin; the only obligation in conscience is to submit to the penalty, if levied. It must, however, be observed, that we are here speaking of laws that are simply and purely penal, where the thing forbidden or enjoined is wholly a matter of indifference, and where the penalty inflicted is an adequate compensation for the civil inconvenience supposed to arise from the offense. But where disobedience to the law involves in it also any degree of public mischief or private injury, there it falls within our former distinction, and is also an offense against conscience.

I have now gone through the definition laid down of a municipal law; and have shown that it is "a rule—of civil conduct—prescribed—by the supreme power in state—commanding what is right, and prohibiting what is wrong"; in the explication of which I have endeavored to interweave a few useful principles concerning the nature of civil government and the obligation of human laws. Before I conclude this section, it may not be amiss to add a few observations concerning the interpretation of laws.

The fairest and most rational method to interpret the will of the legislator is by exploring his intentions at the time when the law was made, by signs the most natural and probable. And these signs are either the words, the context, the subject matter, the effects and consequence, or the spirit and reason of the law. Let us take a short view of them all.

Words are generally to be understood in their usual and most known signification; not so much regarding the propriety of grammar, as their general and popular use. Thus the law which forbade a layman to lay hands on a priest, was adjudged to extend to him who had hurt a priest with a weapon. Again, terms of art, or technical terms, must be taken according to the acceptation of the learned in each art, trade, and science. So in the act of settlement, where the crown of England is limited "to the Princess Sophia, and the heirs of her body, being Protestants," it becomes necessary to call in the assistance of lawyers to ascertain the precise idea of the words "heirs of her body," which in a legal sense comprise only certain of her lineal descendants.

If words happen to be still dubious, we may establish their meaning from the context; with which it may be of singular use to compare a word or a sentence, whenever they are ambiguous, equivocal, or intricate. Thus the proem, or preamble, is often called in to help the construction of an act of parliament. Of the same nature and use is the comparison of a law with other laws that are made by the same legislator, that have some affinity with the subject, or that expressly relate to the same point. Thus, when the law of England declares murder to be felony without benefit of clergy, we must resort to the same law of England to learn what the benefit of clergy is; and when the common law censures simoniacal contracts, it affords great light to the subject to consider what the canon law has adjudged to be simony.

As to the subject matter, words are always to be understood as having a regard thereto; for that is always supposed to be in the eye of the legislator, and all his expressions directed to that end. Thus, when a law forbids all ecclesiastical persons to purchase provisions at Rome, it might seem to prohibit the buying of grain and other victuals; but when we consider that the statute was made to repress the usurpations of the papal see, and that the nominations to benefices by the pope were called provisions, we shall see that the restraint is intended to be laid upon such provisions only.

As to the effects and consequence, the rule is, that where words bear either none, or a very absurd signification, if literally understood, we must a little deviate from the received sense of them. Therefore the law, which enacted "that whoever drew blood in the streets should be punished with the utmost severity," was held after long debate not to extend to the surgeon who opened the vein of a person that fell down in the street with a fit.

But, lastly, the most universal and effectual way of discovering the true meaning of a law, when the words are dubious, is by considering the reason and spirit of it, or the cause which moved the legislator to enact it; for when this reason ceases, the law itself ought likewise to cease with it. An instance of this is given in a case put by Cicero, or whoever was the author of the rhetorical treatise inscribed to Herennius. There was a law, that those who in a storm forsook the ship should forfeit all property therein, and the ship and lading should belong entirely to those who stayed in it. In a dangerous tempest all the mariners forsook the ship, except only one sick passenger, who by reason of his disease, was unable to get out and escape. By chance the ship came safe to port. The sick man kept possession, and claimed the benefit of the law. Now here all the learned agree that the sick man is not within the reason of the law; for the reason of making it was, to give encouragement to such as should venture their lives to save the vessel; but this is a merit which he could never pretend to, who neither stayed in the ship upon that account, nor contributed anything to its preservation.

From this method of interpreting laws, by the reason of them, arises what we call equity, which is defined "the correction of that, wherein the law (by reason of its universality) is deficient." For since in laws all cases cannot be foreseen or expressed, it is necessary that when the general decrees of the law come to be applied to particular cases, there should be somewhere a power vested of defining those circumstances which (had they been foreseen) the legislator himself would have expressed. And these are the cases, which "the law does not define exactly, but leaves something to the discretion of a just and wise judge."

Equity thus depending, essentially, upon the particular circumstances of each individual case, there can be no established rules and fixed precepts of equity laid down without destroying its very essence, and reducing it to a positive law. On the other hand, the liberty of considering all cases in an equitable light must not be indulged too far, lest thereby we destroy all law, and leave the decision of every question entirely in the breast of the judge. And law, without equity, though hard and disagreeable, is much more desirable for the public good than equity without law; which would make every judge a legislator, and introduce most infinite confusion, as there would then be almost as many different rules of action laid down in our courts as there are differences of capacity and sentiment in the human mind.

APPENDIX B

Instructions Applicable
to Criminal and Civil Cases

So much has been written about judges' instructions to juries that a few examples are given here. It will be noted that many of these instructions are definitions of words as used in law. Consider the word *willful*. It has the meaning in law as defined in Instruction No. 5, as distinguished from the meaning given to it by each juror. By defining the meaning at law the judge tries to have all jurors use the word with unison of meaning. This unison could not be attained had the legal definition not been stated.

Other instructions assure that there will be a common understanding of a principle of law involved in the case. Instructions Nos. 16 and 17 illustrate the use of the word *if*. Instruction No. 19 is occasionally mentioned in newspapers as the "Allen Charge." It is given verbatim, as it has become rather famous.

1. DUTY TO LISTEN

It is impossible for a jury to deliver a true, conscientious, and proper verdict in a case where they do not listen to the charge of the court. It is not only a matter of duty, but it is a matter of respect to the judge, that the jurors will do their best to understand the law as he gives it in his charge. The law is a difficult proposition; lawyers do not understand it perfectly; and courts conscientiously differ about what it is. But you must take the law as given to you by the judge. The responsibility of finding the truth of a case rests upon your conscience. The responsibility of giving you the true law of a case rests upon me [the judge].

2. INFERENCE

The permissible drawing of an inference by a jury is a process of reasoning whereby from facts admitted or established by the evidence, including expert testimony, or from common knowledge and experience, a reasonable conclusion may be drawn that a further fact is established.

3. PRESUMPTION

A presumption is an inference of a fact not known, arising from its necessary or usual connection with others which are known.

4. MALICE

Practically, jurymen never deal with express malice. There is no express evidence of malice given to them. Malice is an intent of mind and heart. There is never presented to a jury direct evidence of what was the intent of the man's heart at the time. He is the only possible direct witness to that. The existence or nonexistence of malice is an inference to be drawn by the jury from all the facts in the case.

5. WILLFULNESS

An intentional disregard of a known duty necessary to the safety of the person or property of another, and an entire absence of care for the life, person or property of another, such as exhibits a conscious indifference to consequence, makes a case of constructive or legal "willfulness" so as to charge the person whose duty it was to exercise care with the consequence of a willful injury.

6. RECKLESSNESS

By "reckless" is meant more than negligence. It means proceeding without heed or concern for consequence. It implies no care, coupled with a disregard for consequences.

7. FALSE TESTIMONY

If you believe that any witness has willfully testified falsely to any material fact in this case, in respect to which such witness could not be presumed liable to mistake, you may give no credit to any alleged fact depending upon the statement alone of such witness.

8. OPINION OF JUDGE

You are not to allow yourselves to be influenced by any opinion which you may think I have formed upon any facts in this case. I have not intended to express any opinion; and if you should have gathered that I have any opinion whatever on any fact, you will disregard that, because you are the sole judges of the facts, and my opinion is not to be taken by you.

9. CIRCUMSTANTIAL EVIDENCE

While the plaintiff must prove his case by the preponderance of the evidence, still the proof need not be direct evidence of people who saw the occurrence which is sought to be proved; but the facts may also be proved by circumstantial evidence— that is, by proof of circumstances, if any, such as to give rise to a reasonable inference in the minds of the jury of the truth of the facts alleged and sought to be proved, provided such circumstances, together with all the evidence in the case, constitute a preponderance of the evidence.

10. CARE FOR SELF

A person is required to exercise for his own safety such conduct, care and caution as a reasonably prudent and cautious person would have exercised under the same or like conditions and circumstances which surrounded him at the time. He is not required to use extraordinary care.

11. NEGLIGENCE

"Negligence" is the omission to do something which a reasonable man, guided upon those considerations which ordinarily regulate the conduct of human affairs, would do, or doing something which a prudent and reasonable man would not do— provided, of course, that the party whose conduct is in ques-

190

tion is already in a situation that brings him under the duty of taking care.

12. GROSS NEGLIGENCE

Gross negligence is the want or absence of, or failure to exercise even slight care or diligence; it is the want of that care and diligence which even careless, thoughtless or inattentive persons are accustomed to exercise; it is the failure to take such care as a person of common sense and reasonable skill in like business, but of careless habits, would observe in avoiding injury to his own person or life under circumstances of equal or similar danger; it is a degree of negligence materially greater than ordinary negligence; it must be understood as meaning a greater want of care than is implied by the term, "ordinary negligence."

13. PROXIMATE CAUSE

The term "proximate cause," as that term is used, means a moving and efficient cause, without which the injury in question would not have happened. An act or omission becomes a proximate cause of an injury whenever such injury is the natural and probable consequence of the act or omission in question and one that ought to have been foreseen by a person of ordinary care and prudence in the light of attending circumstances. It need not be the sole cause, but it must be a concurring cause which contributed to the production of the result in question and, but for which, the said result would not have occurred.

14. DAMAGES, TORT

If, under the court's instruction you find plaintiff entitled to a verdict, you will consider, in fixing the amount of the award, these elements of damage. The reasonable value, not exceeding the cost to plaintiff, of the examinations, attention and care by physicians and surgeons, reasonably required, and actually given in treatment of plaintiff and reasonably certain to be required, and to be given, in his future treatment, if any, and including X-ray pictures reasonably necessary; the reasonable cost, not exceeding the cost to plaintiff of services of nurses, attendants, hospital accommodations and care, and ambulance service, reasonably required and actually given, in the treatment of plaintiff, and reasonably certain to be required, and to be given, in his future treatment, if any; the reasonable value of any disfigurement to plaintiff; and the reasonable value of the time lost by plaintiff since his injury wherein he has been unable to pursue his occupation. In determining loss of earning power you should consider his past earning capacity, his actual earnings and find what he was reasonably certain to have earned in the time lost had he not been disabled. You will award to him also such sum as will reasonably compensate him for the pain, discomfort and mental anguish suffered by him and approximately resulting from the injury in question and for such as he is reasonably certain to suffer in the future from the same cause.

15. CONTRACT

"Contract" is an agreement between two or more parties, preliminary steps in the making of which are an offer by one and acceptance by the other, and in which the minds of the parties meet and concur in understanding the terms. Contract includes not only promises set forth in express words, but, in addition, all such implied provisions as are indispensable to effectuate intention of parties and arise from language of contract and circumstances under which it was made.

16. PREPONDERANCE OF EVIDENCE

A preponderance of the evidence means the greater weight of evidence; but this is not determined solely by the number of witnesses testifying in relation to any fact or state of facts. It means that the testimony of the party on whom the burden rests must have greater weight in your estimation, must have a more convincing effect than that opposed to it. If, in your opinion, the testimony on any essential point is evenly balanced, then the party on whom the burden rests to prove the same by a preponderance of the evidence, must be deemed to have failed in regard thereto.

17. SELF-DEFENSE

If the jury shall find from the evidence that the prosecuting witness made the first assault without the right to do so, and that the defendant had good reason to believe, and did believe, that complainant was about to do him some great bodily harm, then the defendant had the right to meet such assault by the use of such force and means as were reasonable and necessary to protect himself from such assault, and, if the jury shall believe from the evidence that the defendant acted in self-defense, as herein explained, they will find him not guilty.

18. REASONABLE DOUBT

A reasonable doubt is a doubt of guilt, reasonably arising from the failure of the evidence to convince the minds of the jury. It reasonably arises from the failures of the evidence introduced in the trial of the case. It does not mean a doubt based on conjecture or imagination, but a reasonable doubt is one for which a good reason could be given. It means a real, solid, sensible doubt. It is a doubt which is reasonable in view of all the testimony.

19. THE "ALLEN CHARGE"

This instruction was given after the jury had been out for several hours. The foreman reported that the jury could not agree on a verdict. The judge then delivered this instruction. The jury, after further deliberations, found the accused guilty. The charge has become famous because it expresses the limit of persuasion which a judge can use.

Although the verdict to which a juror agrees must, of course, be his own verdict, the result of his own convictions, and not a mere acquiescence in the conclusion of his fellows, yet, in order to bring twelve minds to a unanimous result, you must examine the questions submitted to you with candor and with a proper regard and deference to the opinions of each other.

You should consider that the case must at some time be decided; that you are selected in the same manner, and from the same source, from which any future jury must be; and there is no reason to suppose that the case will ever be submitted to twelve men more intelligent, more impartial, or more competent to decide it, or that more or clearer evidence will be produced on the one side or the other. And with this view, it is your duty to decide the case, if you can conscientiously do so. In order to make a decision more practicable, the law imposes the burden of proof on one party or the other, in all cases. In the present case, the burden of proof is upon the commonwealth to establish every part of it, beyond a reasonable doubt; and if, in any part of it, you are left in doubt, the defendant is entitled to the benefit of the doubt, and must be acquitted. But, in conferring together, you ought to pay proper respect to each other's opinions and listen, with a disposition to be convinced, to each other's arguments. And, on the other hand, if much the greater number of your panel are for a conviction, a dissenting juror should consider whether a doubt in his own mind is a reasonable one, which makes no impression upon the minds of so many men—equally honest, equally intelligent with himself and who have heard the same evidence, with the same attention, with an equal desire to arrive at the truth, and under the sanction of the same oath. And, on the other hand, if a majority are for acquittal, the minority ought to seriously ask themselves whether they may not reasonably, and ought not, to doubt the correctness of a judgment which is not concurred in by most of those with whom they are associated, and distrust the weight or sufficiency of that evidence which fails to carry conviction to the minds of their fellows.[1]

[1] Commonwealth v. Tuey, 8 Cush. 1, 61 Mass. 1 (1852).

APPENDIX C

Notes on Provisions for Jury Trials from State Constitutions

THE right of jury trial is stated to be inviolate, or to be secured, or to remain, or to be preserved without distinction between civil and criminal trials, in all fifty state constitutions except those of Colorado, Indiana, Louisiana, North Carolina, Wyoming, and Utah.

The right is stated to be inviolate in criminal cases in Colorado and Wyoming; inviolate in capital cases in Utah; and inviolate or sacred in civil cases in Indiana and North Carolina.

To further secure freedom of the press, the jury is made judge of the law and the facts, with the advice of the trial judge, in trials for criminal libel in nineteen state constitutions.

The constitutions of the following states provide for variation in the right to trial by jury as follows:

ALASKA: Right preserved if amount in suit exceeds 250 dollars. Legislature may provide for verdicts in civil actions by not less than ¾ vote, and in courts not of record for jury of 6 to 12.

ARIZONA: The legislature may provide that jury may be less than 12 in courts not of record and that verdict may be by 9 or more in civil actions in courts of record where parties consent.

ARKANSAS: In civil cases verdict by 9 or more jurors may be accepted.

CALIFORNIA: In civil actions jury may render verdict on ¾ vote. In civil actions and misdemeanor trials parties may agree on any number less than 12.

COLORADO: In civil actions in all courts, or criminal cases in courts not of record, number may be less than 12 as prescribed by law.

FLORIDA: The legislature may fix the number of jurors in any court to not less than six.

GEORGIA: General Assembly may provide that juries may be not less than 5 in courts other than Superior Court.

HAWAII: Right preserved if amount in suit exceeds one hundred dollars. Legislature may provide for verdicts by not less than $3/4$ vote.

IDAHO: In civil actions $3/4$ of jurors may render verdict. In misdemeanor cases legislature may provide for verdicts on $5/6$ vote. In civil actions and misdemeanor trials jurors may be any number less than 12 when parties agree.

ILLINOIS: Legislature may provide that in civil actions before a Justice the number of jurors may be less than 12.

INDIANA: In all criminal cases the jury shall have the right to determine the facts and the law.

IOWA: Legislature may set number of jurors as less than 12 in trials in inferior courts.

KENTUCKY: For civil cases and for misdemeanors in courts inferior to Circuit Court a jury shall consist of 6. In civil cases in Circuit Court the legislature may provide for verdicts by $3/4$ vote of the jury.

LOUISIANA: Where punishment may not be at hard labor, trial is by judge. Where there may be sentence at hard labor, jury of 5; all must concur. Where crime necessarily calls for sentence at hard labor, jury of 12, of whom 9 must concur. Where punishment is capital, jury of 12, and all must concur.

MARYLAND: The jury shall be judge of law as well as the facts in trial of all criminal cases.

MICHIGAN: In all civil actions tried by twelve a verdict shall be received when ten agree. In criminal cases jury may consist of less than twelve in courts not of record.

MINNESOTA: Legislature may provide that after six hours of deliberation, jury may decide by $5/6$ vote in civil actions.

MISSISSIPPI: Legislature may provide that in civil suits in Circuit and Chancery courts, verdict may be by vote of 9.

MISSOURI: Legislature may provide in criminal and civil trials in courts not of record that jurors may be less than twelve and a ⅔ majority may make a civil verdict. In courts of record in civil actions verdict may be by vote of ¾.

MONTANA: For civil cases and for misdemeanor trials in Justice Court jurors shall be not more than 6. In civil trials and in criminal trials for less than felonies verdict may be by vote of ⅔.

NEBRASKA: Legislature may provide that in courts inferior to District Courts number may be less than 12, and authorize in civil trials that verdict may be rendered by not less than vote of ⅚.

NEVADA: In civil trials verdict may be by vote of ¾, subject to change to unanimous by ⅔ vote of the legislature.

NEW HAMPSHIRE: Right preserved if amount in suit exceeds five hundred dollars.

NEW JERSEY: The legislature may authorize that in civil actions where the amount in dispute does not exceed fifty dollars trial by jury of 6 and in civil actions verdict may be by not less than ⅚ vote.

NEW MEXICO: Legislature may provide that in civil actions verdict may be less than unanimous. In courts inferior to district courts jury may be 6.

NEW YORK: Legislature may provide in civil actions for verdicts by not less than ⅚ vote.

NORTH CAROLINA: The legislature may provide for other means of trial for petty misdemeanors, with right of appeal.

NORTH DAKOTA: Legislature may provide that civil actions in courts not of record may be tried by less than 12.

OHIO: Legislature may provide that in civil actions verdict may be by ¾ vote.

OKLAHOMA: Juries in courts of record other than County Courts, 12. In County Courts and courts not of record, 6. In civil trials, and in criminal trials for less than felonies, vote by ¾.

OREGON: In criminal trials in Circuit Court, vote of 10 may give a verdict, except first-degree murder. In civil cases vote of ¾.

SOUTH CAROLINA: In civil and criminal jury cases in Municipal and courts inferior to Circuit Courts jurors shall be six.

SOUTH DAKOTA: Legislature may provide that in any court not of record, jury may be less than 12 and decision in civil trials by ¾ vote.

TEXAS: In civil actions and in criminal trials below felony, in District Courts 9 may make a verdict. Juries in County Courts shall be 6.

UTAH: In courts of general jurisdiction jury of 8, except in capital cases. In courts of inferior jurisdiction jury may be 4. In criminal trials verdict must be unanimous. In civil actions verdict may be by ¾ vote.

VIRGINIA: Assembly may limit number of jurors in civil actions in courts of record to not less than 5 in cases cognizable by Justice of Peace or 7 in cases not cognizable. Laws may provide for less than 12, but not less than 5 in trial of offenses, not felonies; and may classify such and set number of jurors for each.

WASHINGTON: Legislature may provide that in courts not of record, less than 12, and that the verdict may be by 9 or more in civil actions in courts of record.

WEST VIRGINIA: In civil trials before a justice the jury may be six.

WISCONSIN: Legislature may provide that in civil actions verdicts may be based on specific number of votes not less than ⅚.

WYOMING: Legislature may provide that in civil trials in all courts and trials in criminal courts not of record, number may be less than 12.

Index

Admissibility, 78
Affirmative, 108
  defense, 94
  side, 19, 68, 91, 93
Alaska, 195
Allen Charge, the, 101, 193
Alternate jurors, 37
Amendments to the Constitution
  of the United States, 12, 13,
  15, 23, 28, 41, 62, 63, 137,
  156
  Eighteenth, 15
  Fifth, 6, 12, 41, 43, 62, 136, 137
  Fourteenth, 13, 23, 28, 41
  Fourth, 63
  Seventh, 12, 137, 156
  Sixth, 12, 137
American colonial courts, 8
American colonists, 51
The American Commonwealth, 9
American courts, 95, 163
Anglo-Saxon invasion of England,
  3
Answers, 77
Anthropometry, 35, 36
Appeal, 116
Appeals courts, 18
Appellate courts, 17, 18, 49, 75,
  81, 89, 115, 116, 145, 150,
  155 ff.
Appellate judges, 148
Arguments, 130
Arizona, 195
Arkansas, 195
Attaint, 6, 134, 135, 144, 148, 152

Bailment, 113
Bar, 27

Battiste, 146
Bench, 27
Bias, 32
Bible, 72
Bigoted, 33
Bill of rights, 12
Blackstone, Sir William B., 9, 45,
  166, 169-187
Blue Ribbon Jury, 38
Brailsford, 146
Brain, human, 126 ff.
Brief, 155
British Workman's Compensation
  Act, 160
Bryce, Lord James, 9
Burden of proof, 49, 69
Bushell, Juror, 7

California, 195
Capital cases, 100
Care for self, 190
Case, 67
Cause, proximate, 191
Celtic invasion of England, 3
Challenge, 28, 29, 31, 33
  for cause, 31
  peremptory, 33
Charge, 113
  Allen, 101, 193
Circuit Court of Appeals, 17, 160
Circuit courts, 17
Civil case, 91, 94, 100, 122, 124,
  131, 145, 152
Civil trials, 45, 48, 69
Clerk of the court, 27
Code, criminal, 118
Colorado, 195

Commentaries on the Common Law, 9, 10, 169-187
Commissioners, jury, 21
Common law, the, 4, 13, 15, 22, 38, 44, 61, 64, 65, 72, 75, 93, 95, 99, 113, 114, 118, 134, 143, 152, 156, 158, 161, 162
Common law courts, 18
Common law, English, 163
Common pleas, court of, 136
Communication, privileged, 64, 65
Community justice, 141, 144
Competent, 73, 75
Complaint, 46-48, 91
Compurgation, 4
Conclusions, 78
Confidence, 64
Congress of the United States of America, 10, 12, 19, 41, 44
Connecticut, 136
Constitution of the United States, 6, 9-16, 23, 25, 28, 41, 45, 62, 63, 136, 137, 156
  Amendments (*see* Amendments)
  Third Article, 139
Constitutional Convention, 45
Constitutions, state, 45
Contracts, 56, 192
  actions, 46-47
  oral, 85
Contributory negligence, 94
Counterclaim, 94, 134
County Court, 17, 18, 28
Courts
  appeals, 18
  Circuit, 17
  Circuit Court of Appeals, 17
  City, 17
  civil, 2
  common law, 18
  common pleas, 136
  County, 17, 18, 28
  criminal, 2
  District, 17
  Federal, 12, 13
  magistrate, 19
  Municipal, 17
  Police, 17

Courts (Cont.)
  Special Sessions, of, 17
  State, 7, 13, 135
  Supreme, United States, 12, 17, 23, 28, 115, 120, 136, 137, 146, 159, 160
Credibility of evidence, 122
Crime, 42
  infamous, 44
Criminal case, 94, 95, 123, 131, 145, 152
  code, 118
  libel, 117, 118, 148
  trials, 48, 49, 108
Crosby, Governor, 8
Cross-claims, 134
Cross-examination, 63, 83-87, 90, 95, 102
Custodian, jury, 133

Damages
  punitive, 48
  tort, 191, 192
Danish invasion of England, 3
Decisions, 3, 4, 161
Declaration of Independence, 9, 11
Defendant, 46, 47, 51, 89, 91, 92, 94, 95, 100, 113, 123, 125, 136,
Defense, 92
  affirmative, 94
  negative, 94
De Lancy, Judge, 8
Demonstrative evidence, 79
Demurrer, 98
Depositions, 59, 60, 61, 78
Direct examination, 63, 73
Direct testimony, 73, 85
Directed verdict, 67, 68, 92-94, 98-101
Discovery, 60
Discretion, 29
Discretionary power of the judge, 31, 58
District of Columbia, 41, 162
District Courts, 17
Doubt, reasonable, 49, 50, 111, 122, 193
Duty to listen, 188

Ectomorphs, 35
Eighteenth Amendment, 15
Emotions, 126 ff.
Endomorphs, 35
England, 3, 18, 124, 162, 166
  statute law of, 13
English
  colonists, 8
  common law, 163
  Constitution, 10
Equity, 58
Evidence, 56, 66, 72, 75, 78, 81,
    92, 93, 98, 123, 130, 145
  circumstantial, 190
  credibility of, 120
  demonstrative, 79
  preponderance of, 50, 192
  prima facie, 80
  rebuttal, 94, 95
Examination
  direct, 63
  redirect, 87
Exculpate, 95
Executive Agency, 2
Exhibits, 66, 79, 80, 126, 129
Expert witness, 62, 106
Ex post facto law, 157

False testimony, 189, 190
Federal courts, 63
Felonies, 43, 44, 100
Fiction of law, 16
Fifth Amendment, 6, 12, 41, 43,
    62, 63, 136, 137
Finding the facts, 2
First offender, 70
Florida, 14, 196
Foreman, 116, 120
Fourteenth Amendment, 13, 23,
    28, 41
Fourth Amendment, 63
Frankfurter, Justice, 160
Freeman, 5
French civil law, 14

Gadsden Purchase, 14
Gaynage, 6
General verdict, 134
Geneticists, 36

Georgia, 118, 146, 196
Governors of states, 59
Grand jury, 43-45
Gross negligence, 191
Guilt, 122, 123

Hawaii, 196
Hearsay testimony, 78
Hung jury, 101

Idaho, 196
Illinois, 118, 196
Immunity
  charitable corporation, 162
  law on, 163
  of witnesses, 62, 63
Impanelling jury, 24
Impeachment, 12
Improper questions, 74, 96
Indiana, 100, 118, 196
Indictment, 49, 113
Infamous crimes, 44
Inference, 189
Information, an, 44, 45, 113
Innocence, presumption of, 52
Insanity, 93, 158
Intent, 110, 111
Iowa, 51, 196

James, William, 69
Jay, Chief Justice, 120, 146
Jeopardy, 137, 151
Judge, opinion of, 190
Judges, 56 ff.
  discretion, 31, 58
Judgment, 48, 51
Judicial Agency, 2
Juror
  alternate, 37
  attributes of, 25, 26
  oath, 39, 40
Jurisdiction, 18, 19, 58
Jury
  box, 21, 27, 39
  Blue Ribbon, 38
  commissioners, 21
  custodian, 126, 133
  foreman, 116, 120
  grand, 43-45

201

Jury (Cont.)
    hung, 101
    impanelling, 24
    selecting a, 37
    special, 38
    struck, 38
    system, 166
Justice, 12, 139, 140, 142
    community, 141, 144
Justices of the Peace, 17
Justices of the United States Supreme Court, 115

Kansas, 51
Kentucky, 51, 196
King's Courts, 6

Law, 1, 2, 165, 166, 113, 142
    due process of, 41, 42
    ex post facto, 157
    fiction of, 16
    nature of, 10
    principles of, 165
    rule by, 1
Law schools, 56
Lawyer, 54 ff.
Leading questions, 86, 96
Legal principle, 115
Legislative agency, 2
Legislature, 17, 18
Liability, 122
Libel, criminal, 117, 118, 148
Lies, 104 ff.
Litigant, 17, 28, 30, 40, 49, 55, 79, 85, 89, 112, 120, 125, 128, 149
Litigation, 19, 34, 54, 125
Louisiana, 14, 118, 196
Louisiana Purchase, 14

Magistrates courts, 19
Magna Charta, 5, 41
Maine, Supreme Court of, 147
Mala in se, 42, 43
Mala prohibita, 42
Malice, 189
Maryland, 100, 118, 162, 163, 196
Massachusetts, 51, 162, 163
Material, 73, 75
    fact, 96

Mencken, H. L., 110
Mental disease or defect, 93, 94
Mesomorphs, 35
Mexican War, 14
Michigan, 196
Minnesota, 196
Miscarriage of justice, 153
Misdemeanors, 43-45, 100
Misquote a witness, 96
Mississippi, 196
Missouri, 196, 197
Mistrial, 137
Montana, 197
Motion, 67, 93, 98, 99, 153
Motive, 110, 111
Municipal Court, 17

Nebraska, 197
Negative defense, 94
Negligence, 190, 191
    contributory, 94
    gross, 191
Nevada, 197
New Hampshire, 197
New Jersey, 197
New Mexico, 197
New York City, 8
New York State, 38, 51, 101, 127, 197
Ninth Commandment, 107
Nock, Albert Jay, 120
Nolo contendere, 50, 52, 53
Norman ecclesiastical courts, 8
Norman invasion of England, 34, 44
North Carolina, 197
North Dakota, 197
Notary public, 60

Oath, 72
    juror's 39, 40
Objections, overruled, 74
Objections, sustained, 74, 76, 89
Offender, first, 70
Ohio, 197
Ohio Constitution, 149
Oklahoma, 197
Opening statement, 66, 68-70, 93
Opinion of judge, 190

Opinions, 78
Opposing side, 68
Ordinances, 14, 15
Oregon, 118, 197
Overruled objections, 74
Oxford, Pembroke College, 9

Panel, jury, 21, 28, 29
Parliament, 6, 9, 10, 13
Penalty, 48, 51, 125, 145
Penn, William, 7
Pennsylvania, 7
Peremptory challenges, 33, 37
Perjury, 107
Petit jury, 44
Philadelphia, 8
Phrenology, 35, 36
Physiognomy, 35, 36
Pinar Del Rio, 160
Plaintiff, 28, 45-48, 51, 66, 72, 89,
    91, 95, 98, 100, 117, 123-125,
    128, 133, 149, 153, 155, 163
Plea, 94
Pleadings, 47, 49
Police courts, 17
Precedents, 3, 114, 115, 161
Prejudice, 31, 39
Preponderance of evidence, 192
President of the United States, 59
Presumption, 189
Prima facie, 52
    case, 89, 91
    evidence, 80
Principle, legal, 115
Privacy, 64
Privileged communication, 64, 65
Proof, burden of, 49, 69
Proper questions, 74, 84
Prosecutor, 28, 49, 100
Proximate cause, 191
Psychiatry, 93
Punishment, 48, 123
Punitive damage, 48

Questions
    improper, 74
    leading, 86
    proper, 74, 84

Reasonable doubt, 49, 50, 111,
    122, 193
Rebut, 94, 95, 108
Recklessness, 189
Redirect examination, 87
Relevancy, 60, 73, 75
Remand, 156
Revolution, 145, 146
Roberts, Justice, 160
Rules of evidence, 7

Self, care for, 190
Self-defense, 193
Self-incrimination, 62
Sessions court, 7
Set-off, 94, 134
Seventh Amendment, 12, 137, 156
Sixth Amendment, 12, 137
South Carolina, 198
South Dakota, 198
Spain, 14
Special Sessions, Court of, 17
Special juries, 38
Special verdict, 134, 135, 145
Spectators, 58
Star Chamber Courts, 7
Stare decisis, 157, 158
State constitution, 154
State courts, 63, 135
Statement, opening, 66
Statute, 21, 22, 45, 64, 154
    law, 14, 15, 75, 113, 143
Statute of Westminster, the First,
    5, 6
Story, Justice, 146, 147
Struck jury, 38
Subpoena, 58, 59
Subpoena ducas tecum, 59
Summation, 108
Supreme Court of Maine, 147
Supreme Court of the United
    States, 12, 17, 23, 28, 115,
    120, 136, 137, 146, 159, 160
Supreme Court of Vermont, 147
Sustained objections, 74, 76, 89

Tactics, 95
Talesmen, 37

Testimony, 75, 78, 80, 81, 93, 94,
    102, 103, 106, 107, 126, 130
  direct, 73, 85
  false, 189, 190
  hearsay, 78
Texas, 14, 198
Tort, 56
  actions, 46, 47
  damages, 191, 192
  trials, 108
Transcript, 126
Trials
  civil, 45, 48, 69
  criminal, 48, 49

United States, 14, 42, 132, 166
United States, Constitution of (*see*
    Constitution)
United States Court House, Wash-
    ington, D.C., 129
United States Supreme Court (*see*
    Supreme Court)
Utah, 198

Venireman, 21, 23, 29-34, 36-38
Verdict, 32, 39, 66, 70, 72, 108,
    118, 122, 133, 134, 144, 152,
    156
  directed, 67, 68
  general, 134
  setting aside, 152, 155

Verdict (Cont.)
  special, 134, 135, 145
  a true, 39
Vermont, Supreme Court of, 147
Villeins, 5
Virginia, 198
Voir dire, 28-31, 37, 38, 40
Volstead Act, 15

Waiver, 94
Warrant, 63
Washington, 198
Washington, George, Farewell Ad-
    dress, 73
West Virginia, 198
Willfulness, 189
Wilson, Justice, 146
Wisconsin, 198
Witness, 39, 58, 61, 102, 129, 130
  confuse, 96
  expert, 62, 106
  fee, 59, 87
  immunity of, 62, 63
  misquote, 96
  stand, 27
Workman's Compensation Act,
    British, 160
Wyoming, 198

Zenger, John Peter, 8, 9, 144

SAMUEL W. McCART

before his recent death, was a member of the District of Columbia Bar. During his long career as a lawyer he observed and participated in countless jury trials. Both in court and out, he noted the disturbing lack of knowledge about the jury system. Once, he recalls, he began discussing jury trials with two well-educated friends. "The wife boasted of having sat on juries five times," McCart said. "The husband was then sitting on a jury. I asked them their ideas of jury power. They had no answers." He was determined to find the answers and make them available to the public. This book is the result.